Walking with Wheels

in Bedfordshire and Milton Keynes

Lynda Kynnersley

First published August 2006 by
The Book Castle
12 Church Street
Dunstable
Bedfordshire LU5 4RU

ISBN 1 903747 69 4
ISBN 978 1 903747 69 8

Designed and typeset by Caroline and Roger Hillier
The Old Chapel Graphic Design

All the maps in this book were prepared and hand drawn by
Claire Chambers with assistance from Richard Postlethwaite

Printed by Print Solutions Partnership, Wallington, Surrey

Front cover: Reflections on Caldecotte Lake

Contents

WALKS IN MILTON KEYNES

Introduction

This book of walks is especially for people who use wheelchairs or mobility scooters to get around, and for parents of young children in pushchairs or perhaps on small bikes. It will also be useful for those who would like to take up walking as a hobby or to get fit and would like to know that the routes are relatively straightforward and on good firm surfaces.

PRACTICAL CONSIDERATIONS

Access

The walks have all been chosen for their ease of access with as much information as possible about the physical features of the route, to enable people with limited mobility to decide for themselves whether a particular walk is within their ability. Some walks are on trails that have been specially adapted to make them more accessible but others are on country paths, which have reasonably flat, smooth and hard surfaces. They have been graded from one wheel (easy access) to five wheels (most difficult) – see the Accessibility Grading system on page x for more details.

Distance

The walks vary in length from a mile and a half up to seven miles, with the possibility of extending them to up to fourteen miles. The majority of the walks are designed to be circular with different outward and return routes, but in a few cases there are no suitable return routes and the directions will say to retrace your steps to the start point. A few walks are described as linear and on these routes, you can either do the whole walk, arranging transport at each end, or start the walk at any suitable point, go as far as you choose and retrace your route.

The accessibility and distance sections of each walk give a summary of the relevant information but it is advisable to read the route details before setting out, so that you know what is involved.

Details of how to get to the start point, where to park and where to find refreshments are all included, as well as general information of interest about the area and what wildlife you may see - everything in fact for a good trip out.

All-season walking

If the paths used do not have hard surfaces, they may well be muddy in anything other than dry weather. If this is a possibility, it is noted in the accessibility section.

However, a crisp winter's day is a lovely time to be out in the fresh air and if you would like to walk in the colder months, most of the Milton Keynes walks would be very suitable.

Maps

Every care has been taken in walking out and checking these routes, and in creating the sketch maps to accompany them, and it is hoped that you will have no problem completing them. However, people attempting these walks must bear responsibility for their own safety at all times. In particular, it is always advisable to take a map of the area with you to enable you to get the most out of your walk, to vary or shorten the route if required and to avoid getting lost if you should stray from the route. Some walks follow public footpaths and for these the relevant Ordnance Survey map numbers have been given in the introduction to the walk. Some walks use paths in Country Parks and for these it would be sensible to collect a map from the visitor centre before setting out. For the walks in Milton Keynes it is highly recommended that you take a Milton Keynes official city map with you. This is a very useful large-scale map, available from all leading booksellers, which shows all the street names as well as the Redways and Leisure Routes. For those not familiar with Milton Keynes, the city is literally criss-crossed with

Redways and Leisure Routes, commonly called Greenways. Redways are tarmac tracks, shared with cyclists and shown in red on the official map. Leisure Routes are other routes, often on public rights of way, with good firm, but not always tarmac, surfaces and are shown in green on the map. The Milton Keynes walks in this book all use Redways and Greenways extensively.

We hope you enjoy following these routes and find the descriptions helpful and accurate. However, it is always possible for details to change over time and if you should find that the description given on any walk is no longer correct, the author would be pleased to receive details of the changes via the Book Castle, so that the description can be corrected at the next reprint.

ACKNOWLEDGMENTS

The author would like to give her personal thanks to all who helped her with this book, and in particular to:
Gordon Edwards, who inspired her to write it, suggested many of the routes and approved their suitability.
Claire Chambers and Richard Postlethwaite, who drew all the maps.
Her family and friends, who checked all the routes.

She would also like to thank the following bodies, who have created and maintained routes that have proved invaluable to her in finding walks suitable for wheeled access, and the representatives of these bodies, who have given helpful advice and encouragement:
Arlesey Conservation for Nature (ACORN) as a partner in the Bedfordshire County Council's Parish Paths Partnership (P3)
The National Trust at Dunstable Downs and Whipsnade Tree Cathedral
Sustrans, the UK's leading sustainable transport charity, for routes along the Grand Union Canal and the University Way
Harrold-Odell Country Park
Marston Vale Millennium Country Park
The Forestry Commission at Maulden Woods
Priory Country Park, Bedford
The RSPB at Sandy
Bedfordshire and Buckinghamshire County Councils and The Greensand Trust at Stockgrove Country Park
Woburn Abbey by kind permission of his Grace The Duke of Bedford and the Trustees of the Bedford Estates

Walk Distances

Some walks appear more than once below, because these walks have options of different lengths.

Walks less than 2 miles

Ampthill Park
Arlesey Mill Pits
Dunstable Downs Five Knolls Tumuli
Maulden Woods
Priory Country Park, Bedford
RSPB The Lodge Sandy
Stockgrove Country Park
Whipsnade Tree Cathedral (Dunstable Downs)
Furzton Lake

Walks 2–5 miles

Bedford Riverside
Dunstable Downs and Tree Cathedral
Harrold-Odell Country Park
Henlow and Henlow Park
Marston Vale Millennium Country Park
Stewartby Lake
Tempsford Airfield
University Way, Bedford to Blunham
Woburn and the Abbey
Bradwell Abbey
Caldecotte Lake
Campbell Park
Canal Broadwalk
Emerson Valley
Ouzel Valley Park
Furzton and Teardrop Lakes
Willen Lake

Walks more than 5 miles

Leighton Buzzard to Bletchley
University Way, Bedford to Blunham
Emerson Valley

Accessibility Grading system

This grading system relates to terrain only. The distances are shown against individual walks on page ix.

Some walks have more than one entry in the table below because these walks have more than one option with varying degrees of difficulty.

For all walks:

- Minimum width of path is 750mm
- Any gates have an opening wider than 750mm (30 in). A radar key may be required - see individual walks
- Many routes, particularly categories 3 to 5, may be unsuitable after rain or in winter - see individual walks

Category	Description	Walks
⊛ 1 wheel	Hard, flat surfaces over most of the route Level or only very slight inclines	Bedford Riverside Harrold-Odell Country Park Leighton Buzzard–Bletchley Marston Vale Country Park Stewartby Lake Stockgrove Country Park Bradwell Abbey Caldecotte Lake Campbell Park Canal Broadwalk Ouzel Valley Park Willen Lake

Category	Description	Walks
2 wheels	Mainly hard or firm earth surfaces but may be uneven or stony in places May have some slight inclines	Arlesey Mill Pits Henlow and Henlow Park Maulden Woods Priory Country Park, Bedford RSPB Sandy Nature Reserve Stewartby Lake Tempsford Airfield University Way, Bedford to Blunham Whipsnade Tree Cathedral (Dunstable Downs) Woburn and the Abbey Emerson Valley Teardrop Lakes
3 wheels	Variable surface, including grassy May have inclines	Harrold-Odell Country Park Stockgrove Country Park
4 wheels	Surface may be uneven with obstacles to be avoided such as tree roots, large stones, ruts May have inclines	Ampthill Park Maulden Woods Woburn and the Abbey
5 wheels	All types of surface Inclines may be fairly steep or long	Dunstable Downs

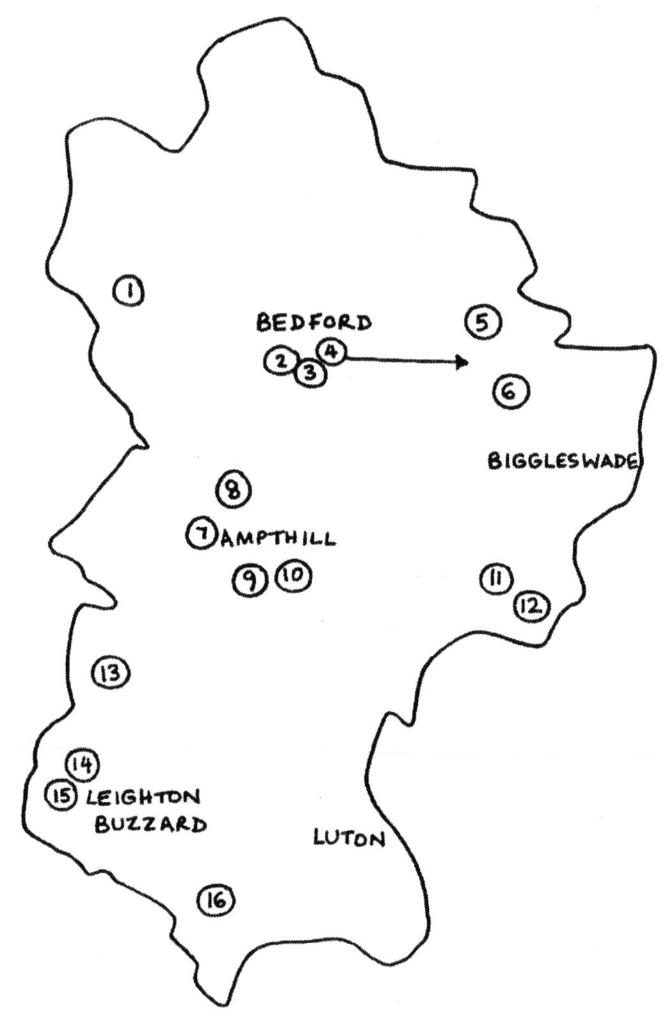

1. HARROLD-ODELL COUNTRY PARK
2. BEDFORD RIVERSIDE
3. PRIORY COUNTRY PARK
4. UNIVERSITY WAY, BEDFORD-BLUNHAM
5. TEMPSFORD
6. RSPB NATURE RESERVE, SANDY
7. MARSTON VALE COUNTRY PARK
8. STEWARTBY LAKE
9. AMPTHILL PARK
10. MAULDEN WOODS
11. HENLOW PARK
12. ARLESEY MILL PITS
13. WOBURN ABBEY
14. STOCKGROVE COUNTRY PARK
15. LEIGHTON BUZZARD TO BLETCHLEY
16. DUNSTABLE DOWNS

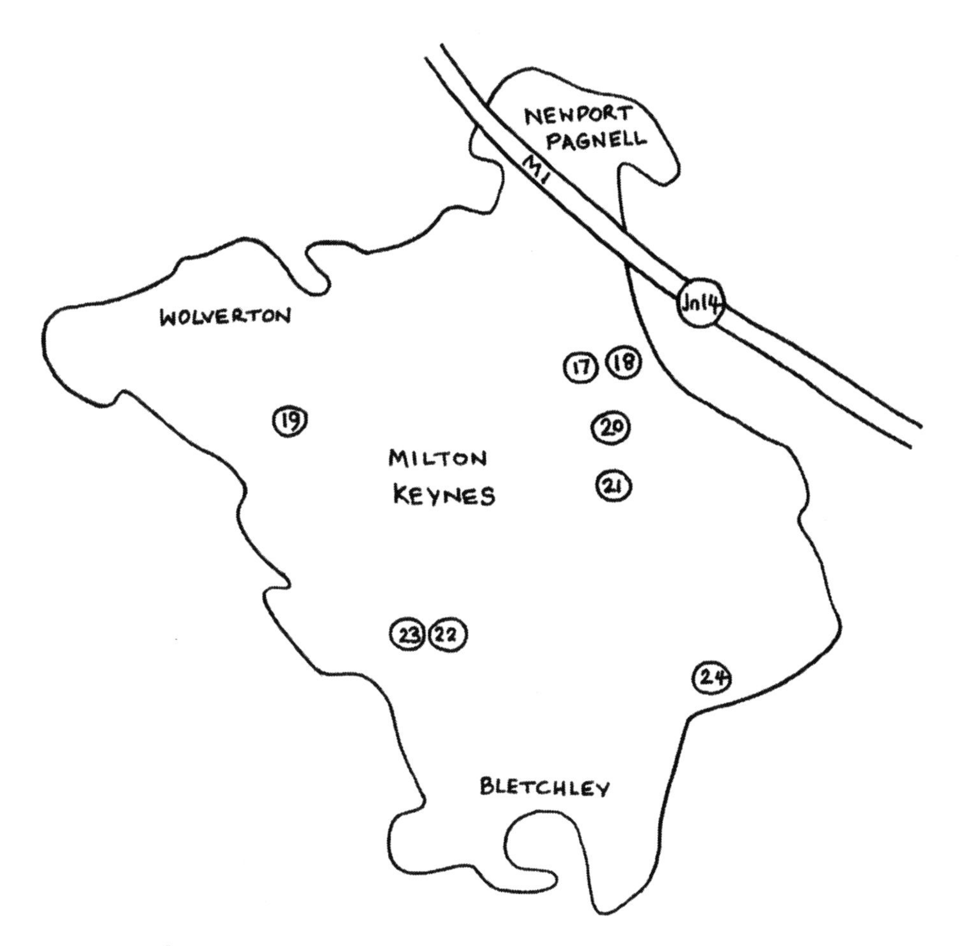

17 CAMPBELL PARK AND GRAND UNION CANAL
18 WILLEN LAKE
19 BRADWELL ABBEY TO LOUGHTON VILLAGE
20 OUZEL VALLEY PARK
21 CANAL BROADWALK
22 FURZTON AND TEARDROP LAKES
23 FURZTON AND EMERSON VALLEY
24 CALDECOTTE LAKE

ABOUT THE AUTHOR

Lynda Kynnersley has enjoyed walking in Bedfordshire and its surrounding counties for more than twenty years and recently came to realise the difficulties faced by less able-bodied people visiting the countryside when a friend, also a keen walker, became dependent on a mobility scooter for getting around. She works in Information Technology but gets out into the countryside at every possible opportunity and leads walks for her local Ramblers' Association group.

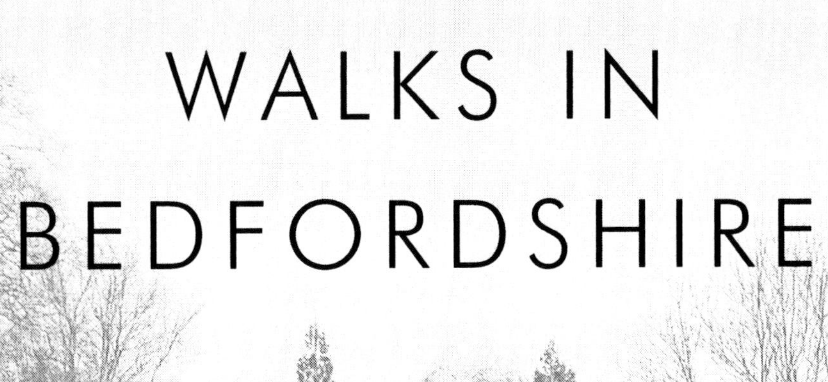
WALKS IN
BEDFORDSHIRE

Harrold-Odell Country Park

Accessibility grading ⊛ or ⊛⊛⊛

The main route uses grassy paths, pavements in the villages of Odell and Harrold and flat firm surfaces and is graded three wheels because of the grassy areas. A slightly shorter alternative is described which uses hard surfaces all the way and this is graded one wheel. The kissing gates throughout the park can all be opened with a radar key to make them more accessible if necessary.

Distance

This is a circular walk of some 3 miles on a variety of surfaces, with alternatives suggested for shortcuts or if particular surfaces are not suitable for you. This walk is covered by Ordnance Survey Explorer map no 208.

Directions and Parking

Harrold-Odell Country Park lies in north Bedfordshire near its border with Northamptonshire, between the villages of Harrold and Odell. It can be reached by taking one of the roads going west from the A6 north of Bedford, such as the Radwell Road from Milton Ernest and following the brown Country Park signs.

There is ample parking in the car park, including spaces reserved for the elderly and disabled. There is no charge for parking but a donation of £1 or more is suggested. The park uses this money for conservation projects and special events.

Refreshments and Facilities

The visitor centre is wheelchair accessible, including the toilets, the 'Café in the Park' and an information room with leaflets and displays. A wheelchair is available to borrow. The Café in the Park is open 7 days a week from 9.30am until 5pm in the summer and until 4pm the rest of the year. The food is all freshly homemade and delicious.

The Bell in Odell is reasonably accessible to wheelchairs inside and the garden is flat, but as it is a very old pub, there is no wheelchair-accessible toilet.

Points of Interest

The walk is very varied and includes meadows, lakes with abundant wildlife and the attractive villages of Odell and Harrold. It uses several trails in the park, which have marker posts indicating which trail you are on, Red, Green or both.

The Country Park is owned and managed by Bedfordshire County Council. It covers an area of some 144 acres with a variety of scenery: lakes, wooded areas, a nature reserve, river meadows and the banks of the Great Ouse. The lakes are old gravel pits, created when the area was restored following sand and gravel extraction after the Second World War. The park is a wildlife haven with over 160 species of birds being recorded. Some are common species such as Canada and Greylag Geese and Mallard but rarer visitors have been seen such as Bittern and Little Egret. There is a hide on the banks of Grebe Lake, which is wheelchair accessible. From here you can watch the wildfowl including, as its name suggests, Great-crested Grebe. Waders and birds of prey are also regularly seen in the park. Along the riverbank you may be lucky enough to see terns or kingfishers.

Various mammals live in the park or visit it from time to time, from the rabbits on the warren to the occasional otter.

You can also see many wildflowers in the park at the right times of year. Look out for Bee, Common Spotted and Marsh Orchids, especially in the nature reserve and for early spring flowers in the woodland.

Odell is a very attractive small village, worth a visit mid-way through the walk, especially if you are visiting The Bell.

Harrold village and surrounding area is of archaeological importance, and remains of an Iron Age farm and evidence of a Roman settlement were found on the site of what is now the

Country Park. Buildings in the village are mainly of limestone, as is common in the area. The lovely old bridge over the river Great Ouse is a Scheduled Ancient Monument; a bridge has been on this site since the 12th century. The church dates from the 13th Century and has a fine 14th-century tower. Other interesting buildings in Harrold include the Market House dating from the late 17th or early 18th century and a circular stone village lockup in use until the 19th century to imprison people overnight. Interestingly, it still has its original padlock. Both these buildings are on the village green on the route of the walk.

THE WALK

Take the bridleway leading from the car park, which is a flat wide gravelled surface. There is a kissing gate on the right here. For the ***Three-wheel graded route***, go through this and immediately turn right on to the Green route to go through the meadows and skirt the lake. The terrain is grassy, rough and uneven in places but it is wide and is a very attractive route going past Kingfisher Water and through the river meadows.

If this surface is not suitable for you, do not go through the kissing gate but follow the instructions at the point labelled ***One-wheel graded route*** below.

Look out for wildfowl on the lake on your left and for rabbits as you pass Rabbit Warren beyond the lake. The river Great Ouse meanders along on your right. If you are lucky, you may see the blue flash of a kingfisher as you go through this area.

Ignore the gate on the left, which leads to narrower paths around the nature reserve and continue through the grassy meadows, admiring the tree lined river bank and the grazing cattle. The cattle are used as part of the management of the park, to remove the coarser grasses to enable the more delicate ones and wild flowers to flourish.

Eventually you will come to another gate on the left, which takes

The Market House

you past the reed beds. Most of the country's reed beds have been drained over the years for agriculture, so those that remain provide very valuable habitats for a variety of flora and fauna. Only sturdy plants can grow in these conditions, such as the common reed, our tallest native grass. The silt trapped by their stems provides nutrients for an abundance of insects, which in turn provide food in summer for the birds. Coot, moorhen and grey heron particularly like to hide among the reeds. Continue past the reed beds to join the Red route. If you want a short cut back, turn left and follow the Red route back to the car park, passing the hide on the way. Otherwise turn right along the bridleway that leads to Odell. The two routes join here, so continue after the next paragraph, which describes the first part of the one-wheel graded route.

A quiet spot by the reed beds

One-wheel graded route

On leaving the car park, do not go through the kissing gate into the meadows but go ahead on the Red/Green Route instead. This is a flat, firm and wide gravelled bridleway, which goes through the middle of the Country Park alongside Grebe Lake. You will see lots of birds on the lake and can visit the hide to watch them. Continue ahead until you come to the end of the lake, where the Red route goes left and continue ahead on the public bridleway that goes to Odell.

The two routes are the same from this point

You will soon come out of the Country Park and reach the pretty village of Odell, with the Bell Public House in the middle. You might like to stop here for refreshments.

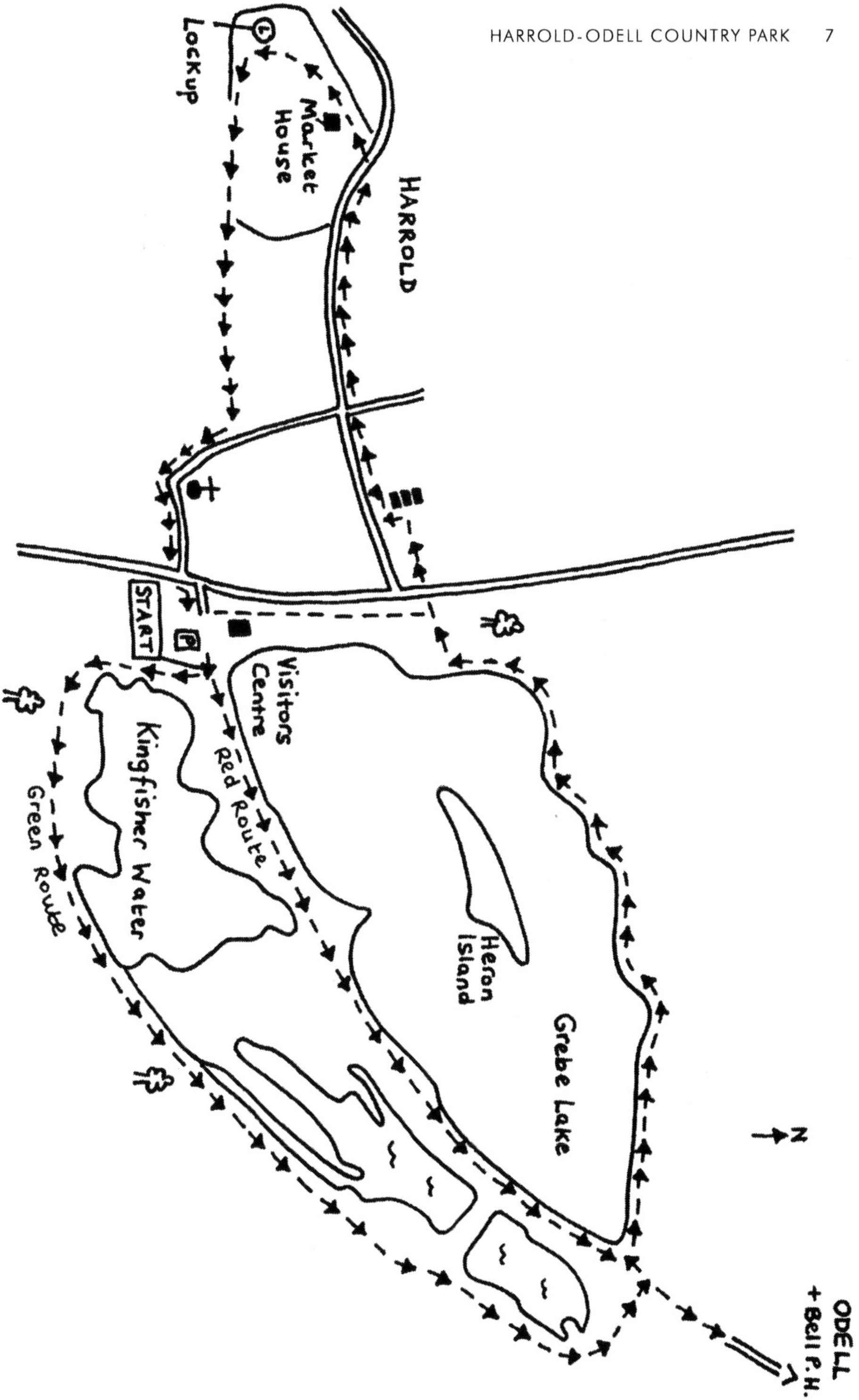

Lockup
Market House
HARROLD
START
P
Visitors Centre
Red Route
Kingfisher Water
Green Route
Heron Island
Grebe Lake
N
ODELL + Bell P.H.

There are no suitable routes from here, so after admiring the village and having refreshments retrace your steps to the Country Park, and at the junction where the Red and Green routes meet at the top end of the lake, take the Red route to the right to complete the circuit of the park. This section of the route has a good firm and flat surface. Grebe Lake with Heron Island in the middle is on your left and open farmland on your right. Continue following the Red route, passing over a bridge and enjoying the views over the water and the water birds, including swans, geese, coot and grebe. When the Red route turns left to go back to the visitor centre, take the path ahead, which brings you out on to the road.

If you want a shortcut back here you can simply continue on the Red route through a wooded section back to the visitor centre, missing out the visit to the village of Harrold. There is also a flat grassy path by the lake accessible via a kissing gate. This grassy path runs parallel to most of this part of the route if this surface is suitable for you.

Otherwise, to visit Harrold with its interesting old buildings, cross the road and go down the surfaced footpath opposite. Turn left when you come out to a point with houses across the path and right when you reach a village road. Continue down this road until you come to the village green with its Market House and Lockup. Cross the road at the zebra crossing and turn right on to the path going round the green and left to go past the old circular lockup on your right. Continue ahead past the lockup away from the green on to a cycle path between houses. Follow this path with good views of the Church ahead. When the cycle path ends and turns into a minor road, turn right, signposted to the thirteenth century church. Go past the church and turn left. You soon reach the main road through the village with the entrance to the Country Park to your left. Cross with care, as there is a slight slope down to the road.

Village Lockup

Bedford Riverside

Accessibility grading 

Easy terrain throughout, on surfaced routes all the way.

Distance

A circular walk of about 2 miles. Bedford is on Ordnance Survey Explorer map 208.

Directions and Parking

This walk starts from the eastern end of the Embankment to the south of Bedford town centre. Approaching from the south, you cross the river and turn first left along the Embankment before the roundabout at Aspects Leisure complex.

There is plenty of parking in the vicinity of this walk but a good place to park is along the Embankment, at the end furthest away from the town centre, opposite Russell Park. Note that there is a two-hour parking limit here but this should allow plenty of time for you to enjoy this walk.

For a longer parking period, you can park in the Aspects Leisure Complex and use the underpass to get to the start of the walk.

Refreshments and Facilities

There are plenty of places to eat and drink in Bedford. Nicholl's Brasserie is on the route of the walk and is accessible for wheelchairs, including disabled toilet facilities.

Points of Interest

This is a leisurely walk, which takes in Bedford's fine riverside setting on the banks of the Great Ouse. There are many things to see: interesting old buildings; the Castle Mound; many different bridges; lots of birds on the water and colourful floral displays.

Bedford is an interesting county town, with lots of historical connections. It was important as a trading centre in Saxon times

River Great Ouse

because of the river, which helped the town to develop. It was given a charter in 1166, confirming its privileges as a borough, and today hosts several **markets**, including farmers' markets, a flower and garden market and regular specialist food and gourmet ones too.

The town has associations with many well-known people. **John Bunyan**, who rose from humble origins to write the world-famous book 'The Pilgrim's Progress', published in 1678, was born in the town and wrote his famous book whilst imprisoned in Bedford Jail. Other famous people who were born or who lived here include Archbishop Trevor Huddleston, Ronnie Barker, Glenn Miller and John Howard.

The **Castle Mound**, a scheduled ancient monument, is all that remains of a medieval motte and bailey castle, the castle itself being destroyed in the 13th century.

The **Swan Hotel**, at the town end of the Embankment, is a former coaching inn dating to the end of the 18th century. It contains the staircase from Houghton House near Ampthill, which is said to be the 'House Beautiful' in Bunyan's 'Pilgrim's Progress'.

THE WALK

Start the walk by turning left along the Embankment with the river on your right. Continue to the end of the Embankment, cross over the white bridge and turn right. You will have Longholme Boating Lake on your left and the River Great Ouse on your right. Soon you will pass the Butterfly Bridge, which has a very distinctive shape, hence the name. It is a recent addition to Bedford's bridges, being opened in 1998 by Prince Charles.

On the left you will pass the end of the Boating Lake from where

Butterfly Bridge

boats are hired, and the Boat House. There is an outdoor café here. Cross Boatslide Bridge, which passes over the weir and you are now in Mill Meadows. You will see the Suspension Bridge over to your right, which was opened in 1888 by the Duke of Bedford. As you approach the Bandstand on the right, there is a bridge on the left, the Royal Engineers Bridge. Cross this and turn right along Route 51, which is less frequented, being further away from the water's edge. Go over Kings Ditch Bridge and continue ahead. You will cross a minor road leading to another bridge but continue ahead here. Cross Abbey Bridge and Rink Island Bridge. You will see Castle Mound and the Swan Hotel across the river and then cross another bridge to pass in front of Bedford Rowing Club. Town Bridge, the former site of the Town Gaol, will be ahead of you and this is about the halfway point of the walk.

Do not go under Town Bridge. It is possible to go further on this side of the river but you will have to return the same way as crossing the river involves steps or very steep slopes. Instead go left past the Moat House and right over

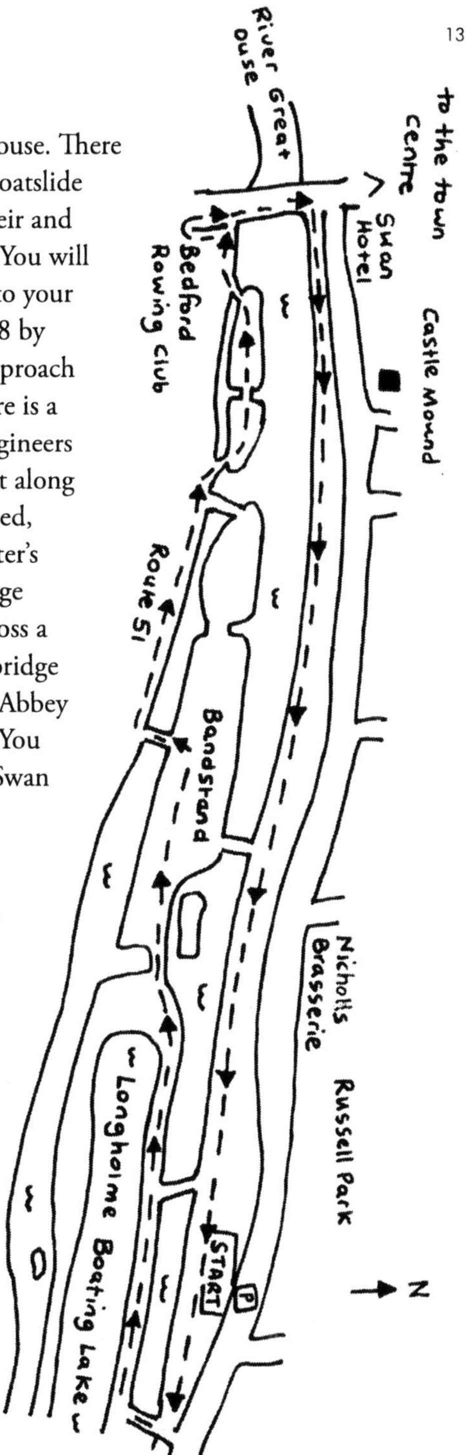

Town Bridge. If you want to visit the town centre for the sights, shops, markets or refreshments, this would be the time to do it. Otherwise, turn right after crossing the bridge and go along the Embankment with the river on your right. You pass the Swan Hotel on your left, then the Castle Mound. There are information boards round the base of the mound and if you would like to explore this further, cross the road (there are dropped kerbs just beyond the roundabout) and go round the base of the mound. If you do this, be sure to cross back again as it is a very pleasant walk alongside the river. Continue all along to the end of the Embankment, admiring the floral displays and waterside views. If you would like some refreshments, Nicholl's Brasserie is across the road just before the end of the walk.

Suspension Bridge

Priory Country Park, Bedford

Accessibility grading

This is a circular walk around the Lake and is on hard surfaces or flat and grassy tracks all the way. However, part of the trail can be very muddy or wet in winter, so it should not be considered suitable for wheelchairs during those months.

Distance

Circular walk about 1½ miles.

Those wishing to do a longer walk could combine this walk with the University Way one, which starts from the same car park.

Directions and Parking

Priory Country Park lies 2km to the east of Bedford town centre. This walk begins at the Barkers Lane entrance, which is signposted from the roundabout near Aspects Leisure Centre.

There is ample free parking in the car park here, which is open at all times.

Refreshments and Facilities

The Visitor Centre at the Barkers Lane entrance is normally open from 9am to 5pm on weekdays and 11am to 6pm at weekends. It contains a public day room and toilets that are accessible to disabled people and it contains leaflets on activities and events in the Park.

Refreshments are available at the Priory Marina Beefeater Restaurant, also at the Barkers Lane entrance. The restaurant has wheelchair access and is a popular spot especially in good weather when visitors often sit outside to enjoy the sunshine.

Points of Interest

Priory Country Park takes its name from an Augustinian Priory, which stood on the northwest part of the site from 1164 until 1541. All that remains of the priory today are the fishponds and an old

Sailing on Priory Lake

limestone wall, known locally as the "ivy wall", although English Heritage has now had most of the ivy removed. It is a scheduled ancient monument, rebuilt in the 17th century, using materials from the old Newnham Priory wall, which stood here previously.

The Park was officially opened in 1986 on a former gravel extraction site. It was designed for a variety of activities including sailing, canoeing, coarse fishing, bird watching, walking and picnicking and is managed to provide habitats for a wide variety of wildlife. There is also a special fishing area with parking for disabled badge holders only.

Priory Lake is used for sailing all year round and is visited by many species of birds at different times of the year, among them heron, mallard, sand martins, house martins, swallows, common

Water birds on the Finger Lakes

terns and cormorants. It is a particularly good spot to see wildfowl in winter. Over two hundred species of birds have been recorded in the park and lists of recently seen species are posted at the Visitor Centre.

THE WALK

The walk begins outside the visitor centre and goes around the lake in a clockwise direction. Start the walk facing the lake with the visitor centre behind you and turn left on to the hard path with the lake on your right. Continue on this path, noticing the bulrushes and reeds in the lake margins, which provide nest sites and food for a variety of birds. After a while you will reach the conservation area where a marked trail, signposted to Finger Lakes, leads off to the left. Ignore this trail but soon after this there is a dead-end path on the left by a litterbin, which, conditions permitting, you can take to look out over the Finger Lakes. This is a peaceful spot where you can see dragonflies and damselflies flying over the lily pads, including the small red-eyed damselfly which only colonised Britain as recently as 1999.

Return to the main path and turn left to continue as it bears right past "the beach", as this area is known. The water here can reach 10–11 feet in depth and is a good place to see Great-crested Grebe, Sandpipers and Grey Wagtails. Over to the left you will see a bridge, which leads to the canoe slalom, where national inter-club finals are held in September every year. Ignore this bridge and continue on the path round the lake, passing an area devoted to fishing swims. Soon a flat grassy surface replaces the hard one. It can be very muddy here in wet conditions but it is possible to skirt the muddy areas. Continue on this grassy path across a meadow until the path bears left and a gravel path goes off it to the right to the bird hide.

To visit the bird hide, take this right-hand path and bear right again after 25 metres. The park is one of the best places in Bedfordshire to see a wide variety of birds, so if this interests you, it would be a good idea to take your binoculars. There is a seasonal information board outside the hide telling you what birds to look out for at different times of the year. Retrace your steps to the main path and turn right to pick up the route where you left it to visit the hide.

You will then cross a culvert and continue into another meadow. Ignore a path going off to the left. At the end of this meadow, cross the sleeper bridge over the stream and go straight on, following the direction indicated by the blue marker.

The path bears left and brings you beside the lake again. Continuing along this path you will see an old limestone wall on your left. This is the "ivy wall" mentioned in the Points of Interest section. Further on is the fishing swim designed for disabled anglers.

Continue along the path until you see the Beefeater ahead, turn right and go through two gates, crossing a minor road between them, to pick up the path alongside the lake back to the visitor centre.

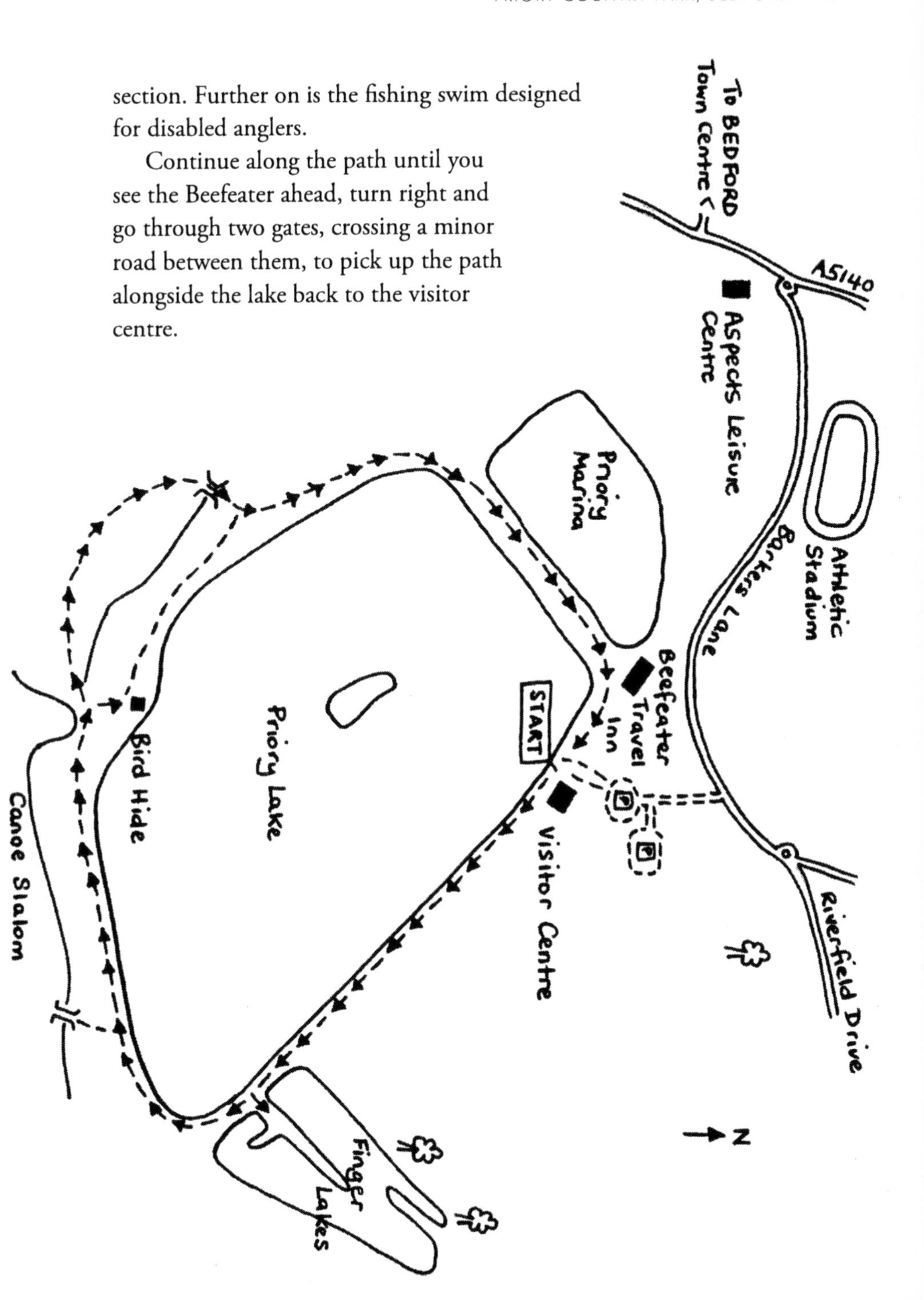

University Way, Bedford to Blunham

Accessibility grading ⊛⊛

This is a linear walk along the University Way and is on firm tracks all the way. The route is flat nearly all the way, except for the slope where it crosses the A421, about a mile from the start, which is quite steep, and a few slight inclines on the final stretch near Blunham. For this reason, it has been graded 2 wheels. If you need to avoid the slope over the A421, there is parking near Danish Camp for visitors and you could start the walk there.

Distance

The route is a section of the University Way from Priory Country Park in Bedford to Blunham, a distance of some five miles.
There are several options:

- Do the whole walk in either direction, arranging transport to and from each end. A linear walk of 5 miles.
- Retrace your route after reaching the end. A circular walk of 10 miles.
- Go as far as you like and retrace your route. In this case, you might like to go as far as Danish Camp (see the Refreshments section) from either end and have some refreshments before returning. A circular walk of about 5 miles.

The route is covered by Ordnance Survey Explorer map 208.

Directions and Parking

Priory Country Park lies 2km to the east of Bedford town centre. The walk begins at the Barkers Lane entrance, which is signposted from the roundabout near Aspects Leisure Centre.

There is ample free parking in the car park here, which is open at all times. The Visitor Centre is normally open from 0900 to 1700 on weekdays and 1100 to 1800 at weekends. It contains a public day room and toilets that are accessible to disabled people and it has leaflets on activities and events in the Park.

Refreshments and Facilities

Refreshments are available at the Priory Marina Beefeater Restaurant, also at the Barkers Lane entrance. The restaurant has wheelchair access and there are plenty of outside tables if the weather is good.

There is also a restaurant at Danish Camp, about half way through this walk. Danish Camp is designated an English Heritage ancient monument and is believed to have been used by the Vikings to keep and repair their boats. There is a visitor centre beautifully situated on the riverbank, a good place to stop for refreshments or lunch. It is a log cabin with a cosy restaurant and extensive terraces overlooking the river, all of which is accessible to wheelchairs, including a toilet. It also offers cycle hire, fishing tickets, boat rides and chipmunks!

Points of Interest

Priory Country Park, the starting point for this walk, takes its name from an Augustinian Priory, which stood on the northwest part of the site from 1164 until 1541. It was officially opened in 1986 on a former gravel extraction site. It was designed to cater for a range of leisure activities and is managed to provide habitats for a wide variety of wildlife.

The walk takes you along a section of the Bedfordshire stretch of route 51, part of the **University Way**, which is the National Cycle Network track from Oxford to Cambridge, managed and promoted by Sustrans, the sustainable transport charity. Throughout the UK 10,000 miles of this network are due to be completed in the near future and a third of this will be on traffic-free paths, which are ideal to be shared by walkers and people on wheels. You can find more details about Sustrans from their website www.nationalcyclenetwork.org.uk.

The route goes close by the village of Willington, mentioned in the Doomsday Book, and home to **Willington Stables and Dovecote**, a National Trust property built around 1541. The

River Great Ouse seen from the University Way

dovecote is lined with more than 1500 nesting boxes and used to stand in the grounds of a historic manor. The stables and dovecote can be visited by appointment but note that there is a step to the entrance. Telephone 01234 838278 if you would like to arrange a viewing.

THE WALK

Follow the route 51 cycle paths all the way. Pick up the route just inside the entrance to Priory Country Park and with Priory Beefeater Travel Inn behind you go in the direction away from the town. A path and surfaced road run alongside each other initially, but eventually the two join. You will pass a bridge to your left and soon after cross a bridge. After a little while the path climbs, fairly steeply for a short way, and then bears right to cross over the A421, and descends on the other side.

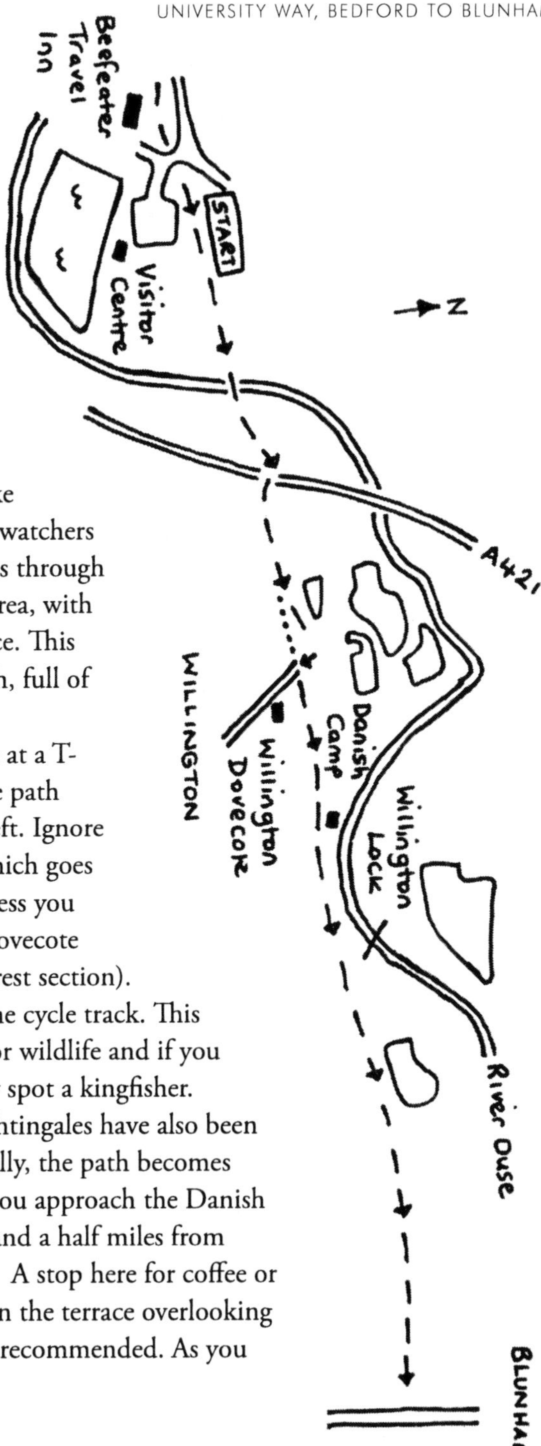

The path then bears left past a lake popular with bird-watchers and eventually goes through a lightly wooded area, with a firm sandy surface. This is a peaceful stretch, full of birdsong.

You then arrive at a T-junction where the path bears right, then left. Ignore the road ahead, which goes to Willington, unless you plan to visit the Dovecote (see Points of Interest section).

Continue on the cycle track. This is a good stretch for wildlife and if you are lucky, you may spot a kingfisher. Barn owls and nightingales have also been seen here. Eventually, the path becomes surfaced again as you approach the Danish Camp, some two and a half miles from where you started. A stop here for coffee or lunch, especially on the terrace overlooking the river, is highly recommended. As you

Willington Lock

pass Danish Camp look out for interesting wildfowl on the lake on the other side of the path.

Continue ahead and after about half a mile the path goes left and then right before reaching the next landmark, Willington Lock. At this point the surfaced path goes right, then left to take you along the path of a dismantled railway as far as Blunham, a further mile and three-quarters. Ignore any crossing paths and continue ahead on the cycle track. There are pleasant open countryside views on this stretch, and a few minor inclines towards the end. The route eventually brings you out into Blunham itself, in a small residential estate at the end of Old Station Court.

Tempsford and Gibraltar Farm Airfield

Accessibility grading ⊛⊛

This is a relatively easy route, almost all on hard, wide surfaces, some of which are uneven in places. A short stretch is on a firm earth surface, parts of which are grassy and may be rutted and muddy after rain or in winter. It is flat and wide however and should be suitable for wheels for the rest of the year.

Distance

3 ½ miles to Gibraltar Farm and back. The route is covered by Ordnance Survey Explorer Map 208.

Directions and Parking

Driving north on the A1, follow signs first to Tempsford, then to Tempsford Station Road. Go all the way through the village on Station Road and across the railway crossing. Turn right immediately after the crossing. There is no parking area, but it is possible to park on the grass verge just after crossing the railway, near the junction of two footpaths.

Refreshments and Facilities

There are no facilities on the walk but there is the Wheatsheaf pub in Church Street, on the other side of the A1 in Tempsford, which is accessible to wheelchairs and has a toilet suitable for disabled access.

Points of Interest

The highlight of this walk is the memorial barn at Gibraltar Farm, on an old derelict airfield. It commemorates the men and women who flew from this airfield during the Second World War, to meet enemy forces in France, Norway, Holland and other countries. The building was built to look like a normal farm barn to fool the enemy but it was from here that equipment for their dangerous missions was issued to them. It contains many photos and moving tributes to

Memorial Barn at Gibraltar Farm

these brave men and women, many of whom lost their lives on these missions. One of these was Violette Szabo, one of only four women ever to receive the George Cross, who left on her last mission from this airfield. Outside the barn, trees have been planted in memory of aircrews that did not return.

THE WALK

Start the walk by going down the minor road away from the railway, towards Woodbury Lodge Farm. The road is initially tree-lined with fields on either side, and then the trees give way to bushes on the right hand side only. At Woodbury Lodge Farm, go through the gate on to the bridleway and ahead, soon passing another house on the left. Go through another gate. The next section has a rougher surface but is still hard. There are attractive open views on all sides over the Bedfordshire countryside.

Just after you pass Woodbury Low Farm, turn right on to a long straight bridleway, on the course of an old Roman road. This is the section that is unsurfaced, grassy and possibly rutted in places and may be muddy after rain, but it is flat and wide. The path goes round a small copse and then past a pond on the right and a sign telling you this route is called the Skylark Ride, a circular route for horse riders. Look out for skylarks, if you are here in spring or summer. The bird is nationally quite scarce but is still often seen and heard singing high above the fields in this part of Bedfordshire.

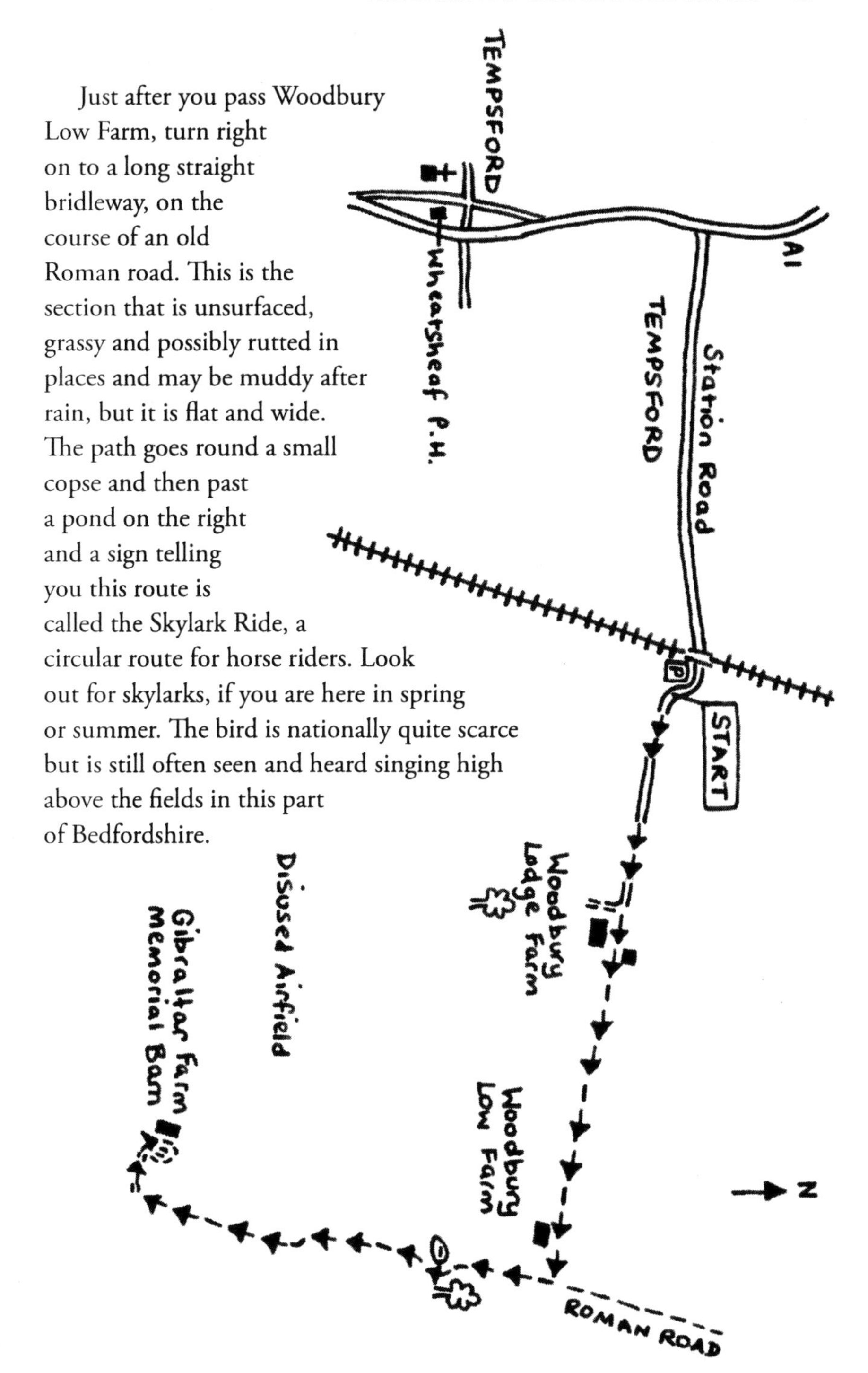

Commemorative tributes inside the barn

The path curves past a small plantation and then you are soon on a hard surface again.

You will come to a footpath T-junction, with a short spur to the left going nowhere, so keep right at this point and continue ahead on the straight path. The disused airfield is now on your right and you can see the memorial barn at Gibraltar Farm. When you reach the barn, you will need to go just past it to pick up the path to its entrance.

Inside the barn there is a quiet and peaceful atmosphere, and it is good to spend time looking at the memorial board, photos and other documents in memory of those who died in the Second World War and had connections with this place.

When you are ready to leave, retrace your route, taking care to avoid the footpath to the right soon after the barn and turning left at Woodbury Low Farm, until you come back to the railway line.

RSPB Nature Reserve, Sandy

Accessibility grading ⊛⊛

Mixed terrain, with firm earth surfaces all the way. The ground is all flat but some tree roots need to be negotiated. All gates open wide to allow full access. Some parts of the route may be muddy in winter or after rain.

Distance

A circular route about 1½ miles long.

Directions and Parking

The RSPB reserve at the Lodge lies just outside Sandy on the B1042 Potton Road. It is signposted from the Sandy roundabout on the A1. As you turn into the reserve from the road, the Gatehouse with its visitor centre and shop is on the left and the car park for visitors is just beyond it.

All visitors are welcome, whether they are members of the RSPB or not, but non-members should purchase an entrance ticket from the shop. These currently cost £3 per adult and £1 per child, with concessions at £1.50 and family tickets at £6. Entrance is free to RSPB members.

As this is a nature reserve and especially if you are visiting the hide, you may want to take binoculars with you.

Refreshments and Facilities

The visitor centre has a shop and drinks machine and there is a large picnic area adjacent to the centre. There are toilets nearby, including ones with disabled access.

There are also plenty of pubs and restaurants in the nearby towns of Sandy and Potton.

Points of Interest

This is a very attractive walk, taking in accessible parts of the reserve and exploring the lovely Italian-styled gardens around the Lodge. Depending on the time of year, you might expect to see and hear a variety of birds as well as many flowers, both wild and cultivated, among beautiful and often very old trees. In spring, there are masses of snowdrops, then daffodils, then bluebells, all carpeting the woodland floor, and you may hear woodpeckers drumming in the trees and songbirds calling. In summer, the wisteria covering the Lodge walls is a beautiful sight, as are the borders in front of the house. This is also the time to enjoy watching lovely dragonflies and butterflies. Autumn brings magnificent fungi and a haze of purple heather and is the best time to see the UK's biggest and oldest Strawberry Tree in the gardens. This is unusual in that it carries its white flowers and red strawberry-like fruits at the same time. Even in winter, you can watch tits and nuthatches on the feeders and thrushes feeding on the bright berries.

An additional attraction during spring to autumn is a flock of Manx Loghtan sheep, which have been introduced to help restore the heathland by keeping invasive plants in check, thereby allowing the heathers to flourish. They can range freely over a large part of the reserve and you may see them at several points on this walk.

The Lodge was designed in 1870 for the son of Sir Robert Peel and became the headquarters of the Royal Society for the Protection of Birds (RSPB) in 1961. The gardens are managed organically and include a large pond, which used to be a swimming pool and is over three metres deep in places. This is home to many enormous fish, which you are bound to see if you go over to the pond. There is also a peaceful memorial garden in memory of those who have left legacies to the RSPB.

The reserve covered some 43 hectares until a couple of years ago, when the RSPB acquired an extra 59 hectares, consisting mainly of conifer plantations. These are gradually being felled to restore the area to heathland and acid grassland to encourage scarce wildlife such as nightjars, woodlarks and natterjack toads. More trails and facilities are also planned.

Manx Loghtan sheep at the Lodge

THE WALK

Leave the visitor car park and go left down the path on the far side of the drive, on the right of the road. Follow this path as it meanders through a wooded area and you will come to a bird hide on the right. This is accessible via a ramp and is worth a visit to look at birds on the feeders and bathing around the edges of the ponds created to make suitable habitats for natterjack toads. Look out for the Manx Loghtan sheep in this area.

After the hide, continue in the same direction, then cross the road at the disabled parking place, and go between two large trees onto a flat path curving to the right. Take care to keep to the path as it curves gently round to the right. This section of the walk is especially attractive when the daffodils are in bloom in spring,

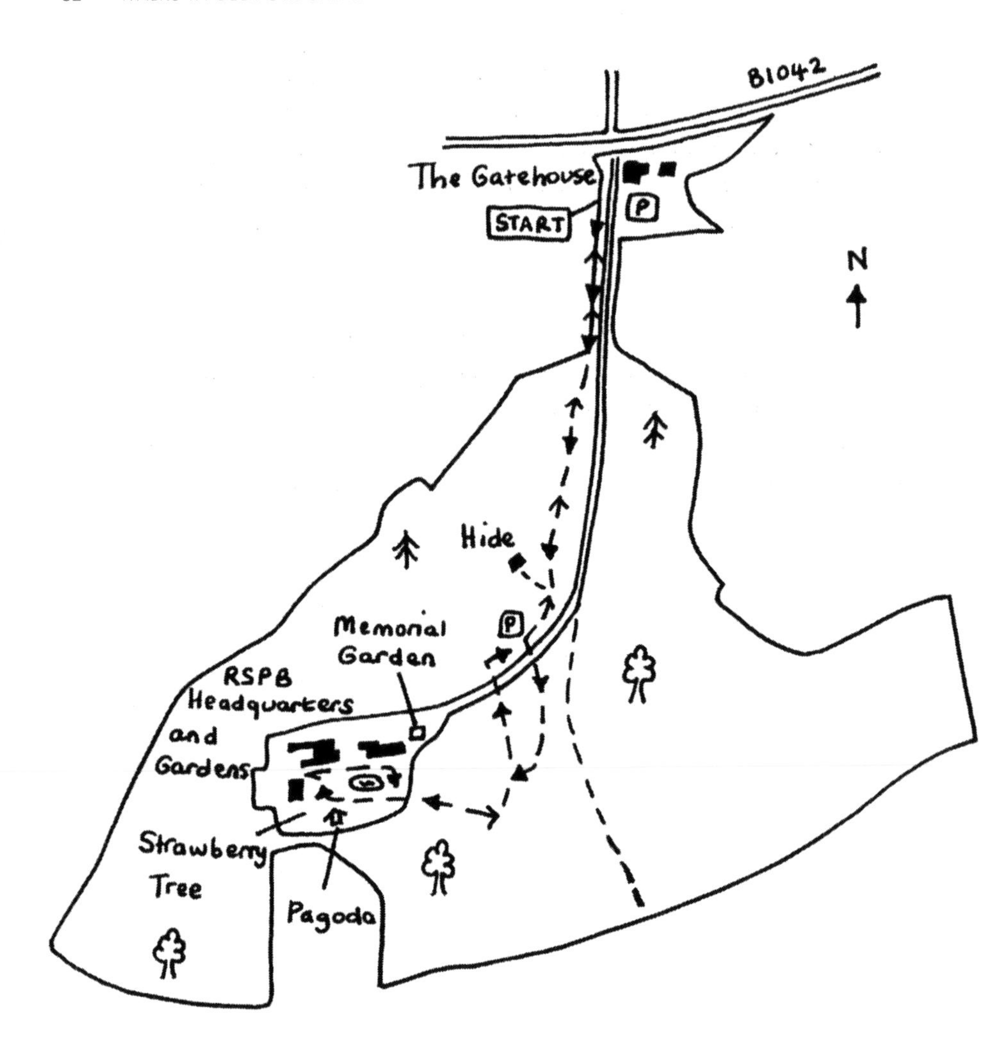

followed soon after by bluebells. Go through the gate and bear left, passing another gate to your left. You will then reach a third gate, which takes you into the formal gardens.

Continue ahead along the paved path, which runs alongside the large pond. Follow the path as it turns right, but at this point, if you find short grass easy to negotiate, you might like to visit the pagoda by going diagonally left over the grass and between the trees.

The Lodge gardens and pool

The strawberry tree is also in this area, nearer to the main office buildings.

Return to the path and continue towards the house. There are steps at the end of this path, but it is possible to avoid them by cutting across the corner of the grass before the bushes. You can then turn right on to the path going in front of the house. At the end of the house, turn left to visit the memorial garden. This is a tranquil spot and well worth a visit. It is accessible through a gate but the paths may be a little narrow. After visiting the memorial garden, retrace your route round the pond and out through the gate. This time, instead of going through the gate you used earlier, take the path that curves left past a car park to the road. Cross the road, go ahead to the path running parallel to the road and turn right to return past the hide to the car park.

Marston Vale Millennium Country Park

Accessibility grading 

Easy terrain throughout, with hard flat surfaces all the way. All gates are accessible to wheelchairs and mobility scooters.

Distance

Circular walk about 2½ miles.
This walk could be combined with the Stewartby Lake one to make a 5-mile figure-of-eight walk.

Directions and Parking

The Forest Centre in the Marston Vale Millennium Country Park is signposted from the A421 at the Marston Moretaine Little Chef roundabout between Bedford and Milton Keynes. There is also a railway station at Millbrook, which gives access to the walk.
There is ample free parking at the Forest Centre. The car park is open from 10am to 4pm in the winter and until 6pm in the summer.

Refreshments and Facilities

There is a licensed cafe within the Forest Centre, which serves a wide variety of snacks, drinks and meals. It has large windows overlooking the park and tables where visitors can sit outside in summer.
The Centre also houses a shop, toilets and an exhibition area, all accessible to wheelchair users.

Points of Interest

The **Forest of Marston Vale** was established in 1991 and is one of 12 Community Forests in England, developed with the aim of regenerating the countryside around urban areas by planting trees. Here in Bedfordshire the Forest team at the Millennium Country Park and Forest Centre is aiming to repair a landscape ravaged by clay extraction for the brick making industry over many years. In

View from path near the Forest Centre

the sixty-one square miles covered by the Forest, they will plant over five million trees in the next twenty-five years: over half a million have been planted already. The Centre has lots of information and leaflets on what is currently happening in the Country Park and it is well worth visiting it before you set off. The Country Park attracts many species of birds; in spring it is possible to see over eighty species here in a day. While in the Centre it is also worth checking the board showing which birds have been seen here recently.

THE WALK

With the Forest Centre main entrance behind you, a Timberland Trail footpath sign on your left and a Swallow Trail sign on your right, go straight ahead to cross the roundabout, through the gate and turn left to pick up the path that runs alongside the approach

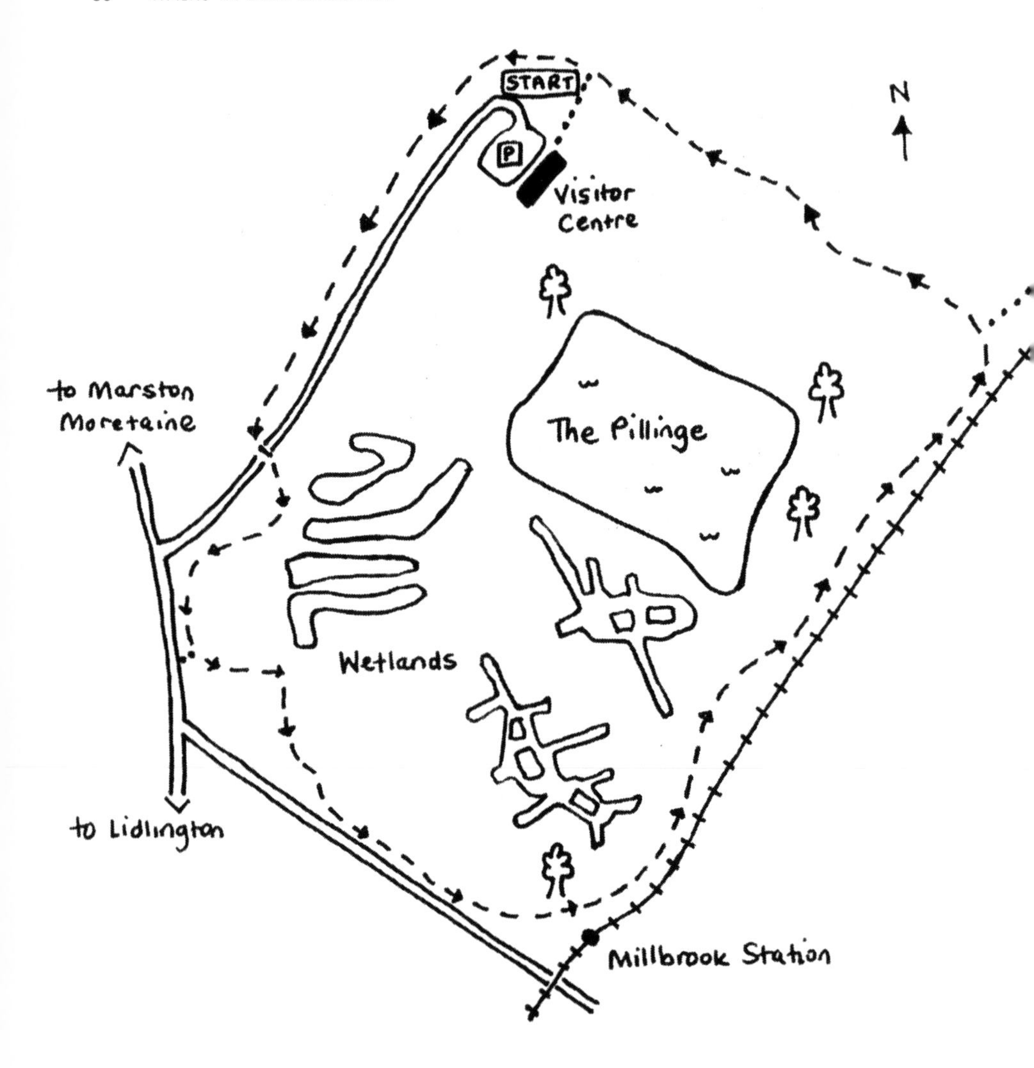

road. The trail is indicated by a board depicting swallows, and initially takes you back towards the main vehicle entrance. Cross this road where indicated and follow the clearly marked trail as it winds its way round the southern part of the Country Park. Iron Age and Anglo-Saxon artefacts have been found in this area, some of which are on display in the exhibition in the Forest Centre. As you go round the trail, look out for the colourful carved benches along

View over the water beyond the Forest Centre

the route, depicting the wildlife to be seen in the area.

After a while, you will see Millbrook station on your right as the trail curves to the left. There are two main trails around this part of the Country Park, an inner Horse Trail and an outer Walkers' and Cyclists' Trail. Keeping to the outer trail, continue along this stretch past the Wetlands Reserve on your left. Eventually you will come to a junction of footpaths, ahead to Stewartby and left back to the Centre. Take the path to the left to return to the Forest Centre. In addition, you might like to visit the Wetlands Reserve. This area has been specially created and maintained to provide a habitat for many plants, insects and animals, including some rare species. There is an admission charge and special wheelchairs are available if required to allow access to the mile and a half of trail around it. It would be a good idea to ring the Centre in advance on 01234 767037 if you would like to reserve one.

Stewartby Lake

Accessibility grading ⊛ or ⊛⊛

Reasonable terrain throughout, with firm earth surfaces all the way. There is an option at the end for a slightly more difficult route, which is graded 2 wheels and has a kissing gate at the end that may not be suitable for larger mobility scooters. This route is likely to be muddy in winter or after rain.

Distance

Circular walk about 2½ miles.

This walk could be combined with the Marston Vale Millennium Country Park one to make a 5 mile figure-of-eight walk.

Directions and Parking

The Forest Centre in the Marston Vale Millennium Country Park, of which Stewartby Lake is a part, is signposted from the A421 at the Marston Moretaine Little Chef roundabout between Bedford and Milton Keynes. There is also a railway station at Stewartby, which gives access to the walk.

There is ample free parking at the Forest Centre. The car park is open from 10am to 4pm in the winter and until 6pm in the summer. Outside these times, or if you prefer, there is a parking area beside the road shortly after leaving Stewartby village but the access gate to the lakeside path here may not be wide enough for large mobility scooters. If you do park here, follow the track round the lake with the water on your right, picking up the instructions in the Walk section from where the route passes the Water Sports club.

Refreshments and Facilities

There is a licensed cafe within the Forest Centre, serving a variety of snacks, drinks and meals. It has large windows overlooking the park and outside tables. The Centre also houses a shop, toilets and an exhibition area, all accessible to wheelchair users.

Points of Interest

Stewartby Lake was formed by the extraction of clay for brick making and the brickworks' chimneys are a feature of the landscape here. Nowadays it is a haven for birds and wildlife and is very popular with birdwatchers; in spring it is possible to see over eighty species in a day here. This interest is reflected in the Forest Centre where there is a board showing which birds have been seen in the area recently. In contrast to this, the lake is also enjoyed by water sports enthusiasts and it can be entertaining to watch their activities from the shore.

The **Forest of Marston Vale** was established in 1991 and is one of 12 Community Forests in England, developed with the aim of regenerating the countryside around urban areas by planting trees. Here in Bedfordshire the Forest team at the Millennium Country Park and Forest Centre is aiming to repair a landscape ravaged by clay extraction for the brick making industry over many years. The Centre has lots of information and leaflets on what is currently happening in the Country Park and it is well worth visiting it before you set off.

THE WALK

The route goes round the perimeter of Stewartby Lake in a clockwise direction.

With the Forest Centre main entrance behind you, a Timberland Trail footpath sign on your left and a Swallow Trail sign on your right, go straight ahead to cross the roundabout, through the gate and turn right. Follow the path as it bears left on the Jubilee Walk, going past a signpost on the right. Cross over a brook and continue ahead on the main track. Pass a marker post on the left and after about a third of a mile, the Jubilee Walk goes off to the left and you should go ahead and take the path to the right signposted Stewartby 2.8km.

Keep to the path round the lake with the water on your right from now on. The poplar trees in this section were planted as a screen while the clay was being extracted and are now home to Green and Greater-spotted Woodpeckers. There are good views of the lake and places to stop to look for wildfowl on the water or watch the colourful sailing boats and water skiers. You will soon

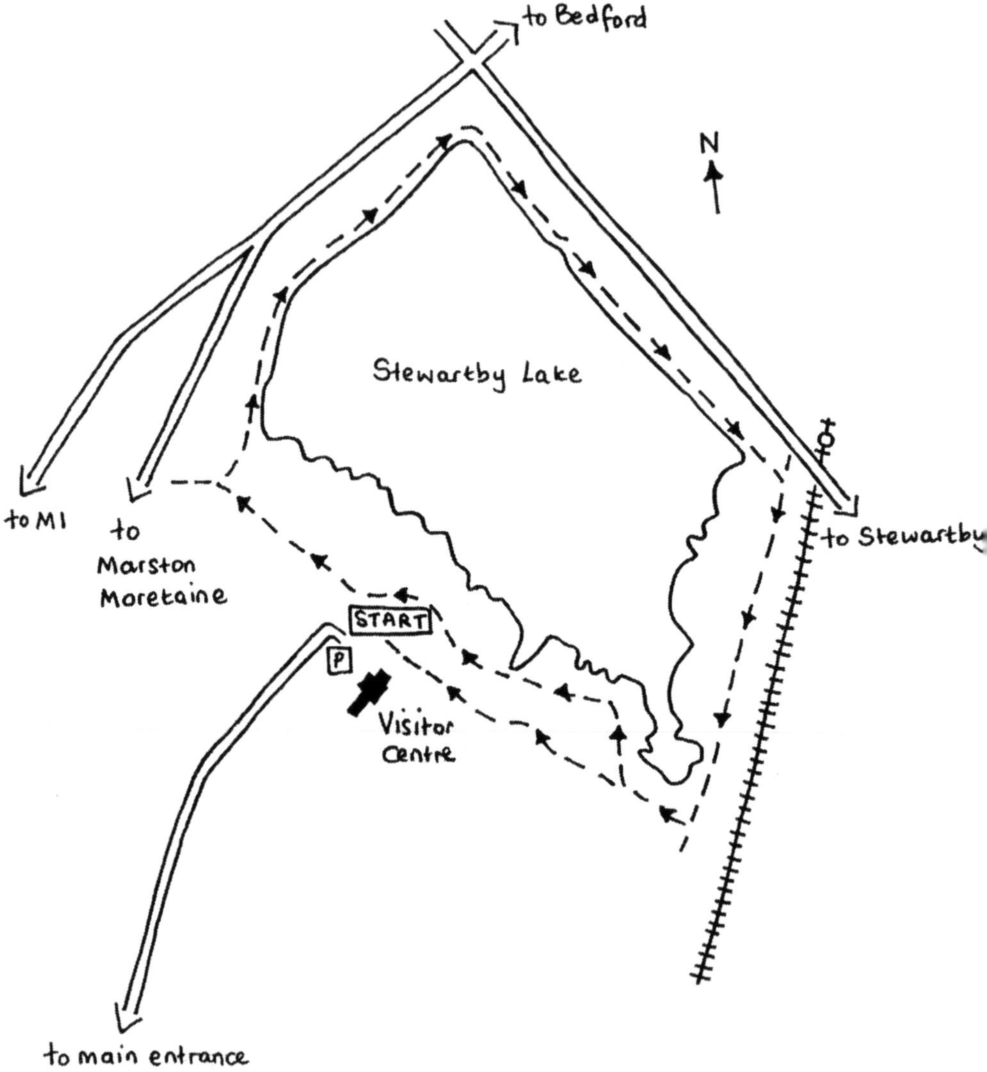

Industry and recreation on Stewartby Lake

cross a wide bridge over a sluice. This is the point where Elstow brook leaves the Lake. Elstow Brook is the main watercourse in the Marston Vale Forest and is used for land drainage and flood control. Continue on the track round the lake, passing the Water Sports club with its sailing boats whose masts are usually clinking in the breeze. Soon after the club, the views open out over the water and to the countryside beyond. Eventually you come to a signpost to the Visitor Centre and you should turn right here.

In a short distance, you will reach a signpost indicating an easy access path to a viewpoint on the right. You can now either continue ahead on the main track back to the Visitor Centre (the easiest and most direct route) or take this path to the right. It is a more difficult route but well worth it if you feel it is within your capabilities. However, in winter or after rain, it can be muddy and slippery and the kissing gate at the end may not be wide enough for large mobility scooters. The track is quite wide and sandy and zigzags as it climbs to a point above the lake with carved oak benches and good

Carved oak bench overlooking the lake

views. You can then either go back down and return to the Visitor Centre on the main track or continue on this high path with the lake visible on your right through a wooded section before the path descends. When the path splits, you can continue ahead on the main path, or you can take the path to the right down to the lake. This path is not quite as flat or smooth as the one it forks from and may be muddier but it does have pretty views of the lake if the surface is suitable for you and the ground is dry. If you take this path, follow it round and the two join in a little while at a point where you can see the visitor centre over to the left and slightly behind you. Continue ahead as the path climbs to come to a kissing gate. This is the one that may not be suitable for larger mobility scooters (see Accessibility section). Go through the gate and continue until you come to a signpost indicating Forest Centre 0.2km and turn left here. At the fork, the left path takes you to the Visitor Centre and the right one to the car park, going left to reach it through the gate you used on the outward route.

Ampthill Park

Accessibility grading ❀❀❀❀

The terrain is a mixture of firm earth and grassy tracks, with some inclines and uneven surfaces. It may be difficult for manual wheelchairs at any time and may not be suitable for other wheels in winter or after prolonged rain.

There are two kissing gates, both accessible to wheels.

Distance

A circular walk of about 1½ miles. The route is covered by the Ordnance Survey Explorer map 193.

Directions and Parking

Ampthill Park lies between the town of Ampthill and the A507 and its main car park is situated near the junction of the A507 and the B530. If approaching on the A507 from Clophill, go ahead, not right, at the roundabout where Ampthill is signposted right and turn right at the next roundabout. At the top of the hill, take the right turn to Ampthill and the car park is on the left immediately after leaving the A507. Alternatively, the Park can be reached by taking Woburn Road out of the town and turning right into the car park just before the A507.

There is plenty of free parking here, including some reserved for disabled badge holders.

Refreshments and Facilities

There are no refreshments in the park but there are several pubs and restaurants in the town itself. The White Hart Hotel in the centre of town has been recently refurbished and has wheelchair access, including to toilet facilities.

There are toilets near the start of the walk but they are in a fairly poor state of repair and do not have wheelchair access.

St Katherine's Cross

Points of Interest

This is a very attractive walk, which includes woodland, parkland and extensive views over the surrounding countryside.

Ampthill is a lovely Georgian town with over 200 listed buildings, and is well worth a visit.

The Park is a remnant of a deer park that once surrounded Ampthill Castle, which fell into disrepair after the reign of Henry VIII and eventually disappeared. The site of the castle is marked by **St Katherine's Cross**, built to commemorate Katherine of Aragon, who was imprisoned there by Henry VIII during her trial

View from the Greensand Ridge Walk

and annulment. The Park was landscaped by Capability Brown in the 18th century and is now owned by Ampthill Town Council.

THE WALK

Leave the car park by taking the track that runs through the Park from the lower end of the car park towards the town, parallel to the road into Ampthill. Go past the cricket ground on your left and carry on ahead when the path bears right to the road. You next pass the football stadium and some toilets and then enter a wooded area. Follow this wide track ahead as it climbs slightly, ignoring any crossing paths. Shortly a wide track crosses the one you are on. Continue on the path ahead, which climbs for a short way until it reaches a broad path where you turn left to come out of the wooded area into the parkland, through a kissing gate with a Timberland Trail marker on it.

Many wide grassy paths cross the parkland. Keep going straight ahead to the top of the hill, which is a gentle climb but over uneven ground. There is a children's playground over on the left. The path bears left along the ridge, and converges shortly with another path. You are now on the Greensand Ridge Walk, Bedfordshire's premier long-distance footpath, which follows the ridge for 40 miles between Leighton Buzzard and Gamlingay.

Away on your left you will see the Ampthill Camp Memorial Cross. This sits on the site of the camp built to train soldiers for the 1914-18 war by their commanding officer, the then Duke of Bedford. From this spot more than 2,000 men under his command left to join the battle in France, where 707 of them died.

On your right, there are extensive views over the surrounding countryside. Look out for Millbrook proving ground, Stewartby Lake and brickworks and Ravensden water tower. The large building you can see below you on the right is Park House, built by the first Baron Ashburnam in 1694.

Continue ahead, past St Katherine's Cross, built in memory of Katherine of Aragon. You then come to a wide track where the Greensand Ridge Walk goes ahead. Turn left on to this track, which takes you back to the Car Park through a kissing gate.

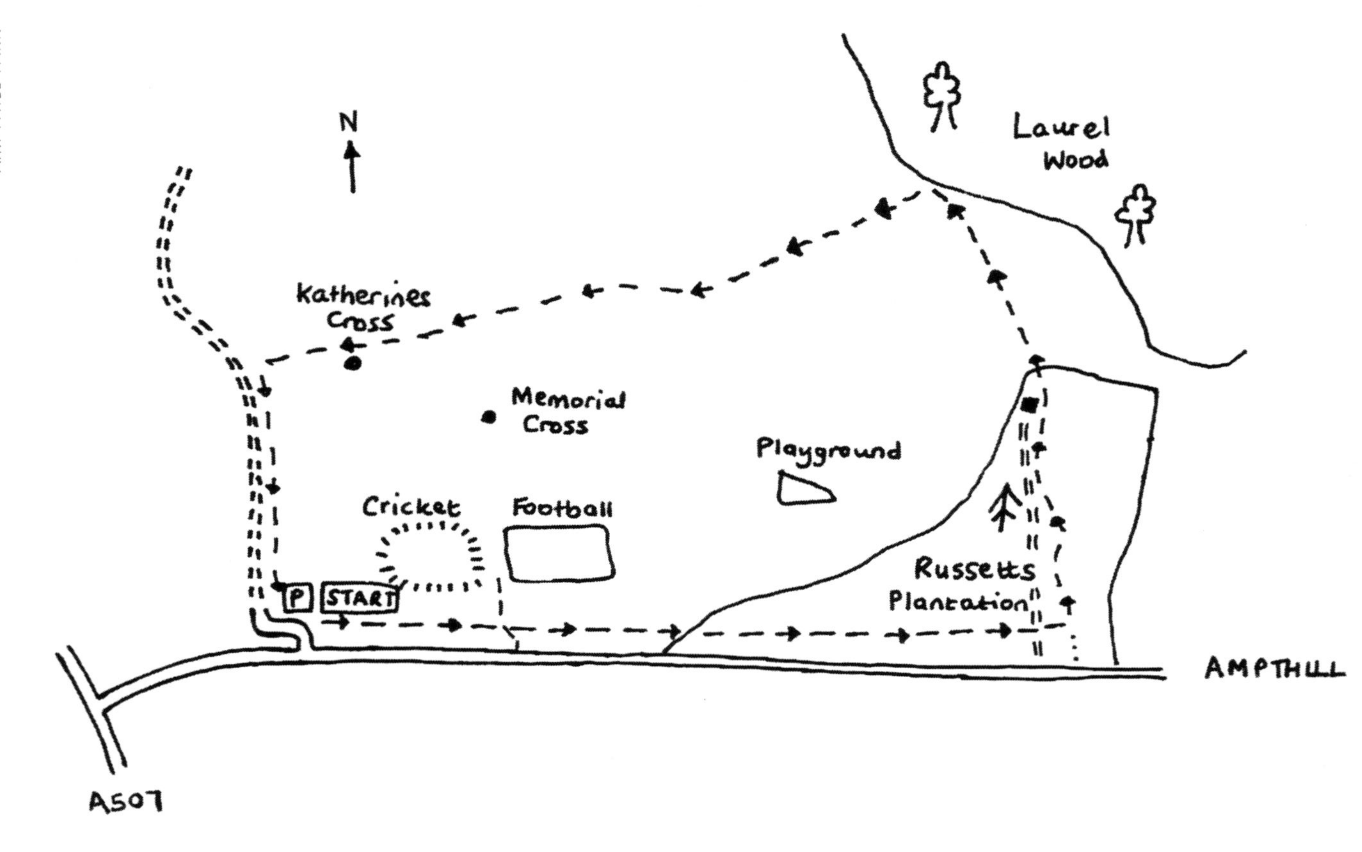
N
Laurel Wood
Katherines Cross
Memorial Cross
Playground
Cricket
Football
Russetts Plantation
P
START
AMPTHILL
A507

Maulden Woods

Accessibility grading ⊛⊛ or ⊛⊛⊛⊛

There is a series of trails through the woods, one of which, the Dormouse Trail, is designated as all-ability and suitable for wheelchair users. It has been graded two wheels because some of the surface is on firm earth, rather than a hard surface. This part is likely to be muddy in winter or after rain.

The walk graded four wheels extends the Dormouse Trail to cover more of the woodland. The terrain is mixed, some on hard surfaces and some on firm and grassy tracks. There are also some inclines. This extended route may not be suitable in winter or after rain because of the soft terrain.

Distance

The Dormouse Trail is a circular route just over ½ mile long. With the extension, the route is about 2 miles long. The route is covered by the Ordnance Survey Explorer map no 193.

Directions and Parking

Maulden Woods are situated on the A6 five miles south of Bedford, just north of the roundabout with the A507 at Clophill. Even if travelling from the north, it is best to go to this roundabout and approach the woods from the south.

Plenty of free parking is available in the main car park for the woods, Deadmans Hill lay-by, situated at the top of the hill coming from the Clophill direction.

Refreshments and Facilities

Apart from an occasional refreshment van in the lay-by, there are no refreshments or facilities in the woods. There are picnic tables at the car park entrance and on the route itself.

There are several pubs in nearby Clophill serving food and drink, including the Flying Horse near the roundabout, which has a

Picnic area at entrance to Maulden Woods

Beefeater restaurant. There is reasonable access, but as yet wheelchair accessible toilets are still being planned.

Points of Interest

Maulden Wood is a Forestry Commission woodland and is the largest ancient woodland on the Greensand Ridge, an area of high ground crossing Bedfordshire. It has been designated a Site of Special Scientific Interest because of the variety and quality of its flora and fauna. In spring the ground is carpeted with bluebells and in its secluded spots you may see fallow and muntjac deer. It is also home to badgers, butterflies such as the common blue and small copper, and many birds, including birds of prey.

THE WALK

The route described is the extended one. For the shorter, two-wheel route, follow the white Dormouse Trail signs.

As you enter the woods from the lay-by, there is an information board facing you giving details of all the trails and information about the woodland. There is also a big sign showing the Dormouse (or white) trail going ahead down a wide ride. However, this walk follows the trail in the opposite direction, so turn left at the information board on to a wide ride parallel to the road. You will see marker posts along the path with a white band around them while you are on the white route. Stay on this wide path, following it as it goes to the right and ignoring the path with red marker posts to the left just after the bend. In a short distance the main path bears left but the white trail goes ahead. At this point continue on the main path going left instead of following the white trail. We will pick this

Path through the trees

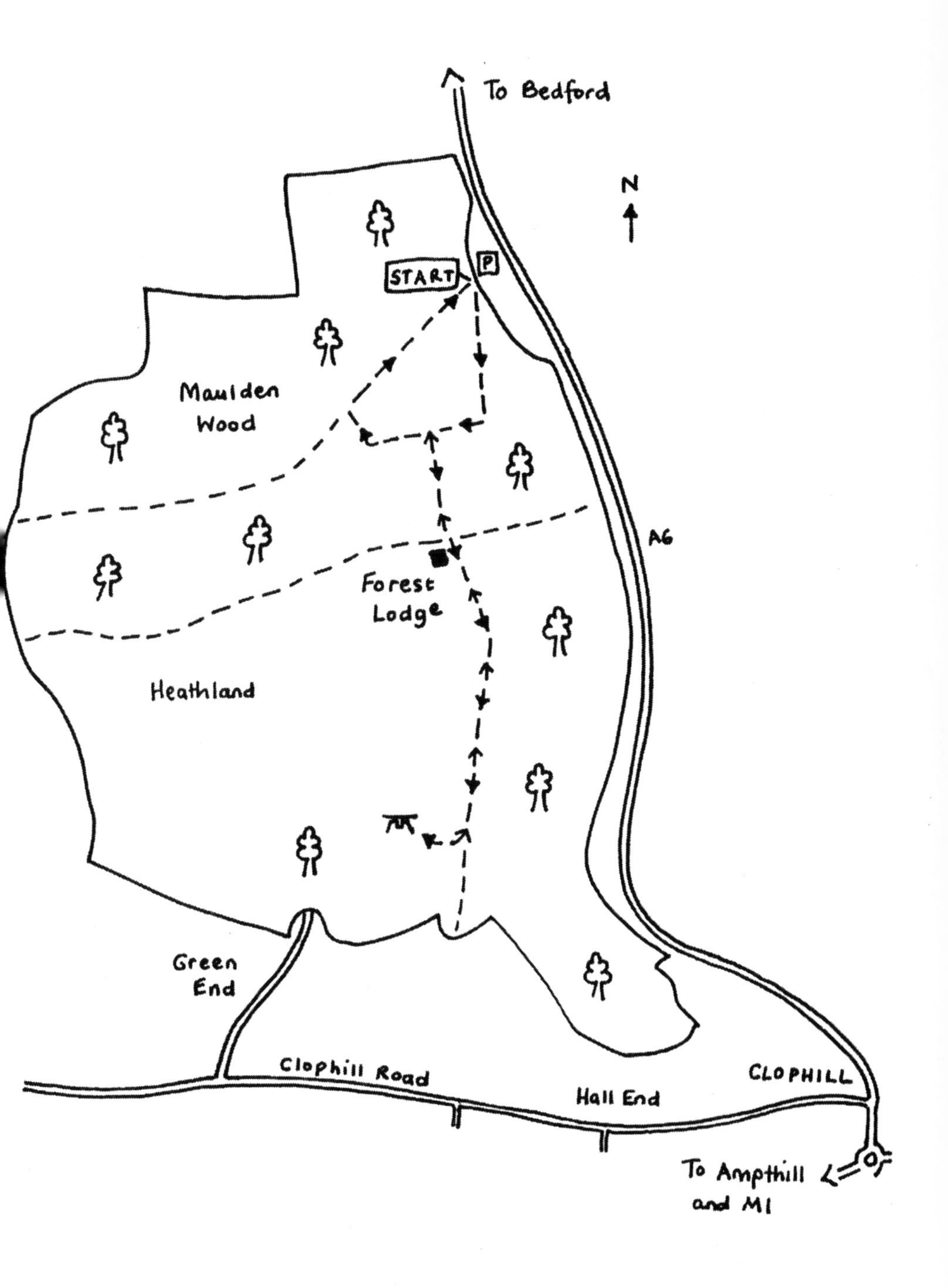
To Bedford
N
START
P
Maulden Wood
A6
Forest Lodge
Heathland
Green End
Clophill Road
Hall End
CLOPHILL
To Ampthill and M1

up again later. A signed public bridleway crosses the route just after it turns left, but ignore this and continue ahead.

After about a quarter of a mile you will see a house, Forest Lodge, on your right. Before the house there is a barrier, which may be across the path. If so, it can sometimes be lifted off its peg in order to pass through but, if not, a gap has been made by the side of the gate to enable wheeled access. Just after the house is another barrier across the path, with a fence on the left and a gap on the right, which has also been made accessible for wheeled access. Go through this gap and continue ahead on this wide ride through the woodland. On your left is a steep bank, which is a haze of bluebells in spring. The ride becomes more undulating and there are some paths that cross it and some that lead off from it. Ignore them all and continue ahead on the wide ride for about half a mile until you come to a large footpath crossroads just after a climb. The path ahead at this point slopes downhill and has a red marker post on the left. The path to the right is wide and grassy. You should leave the wide ride here and turn right on to this path. Continue as the path curves right and comes out at a clearing with benches and a table, a good place for a break or a picnic.

The path ahead after the clearing has a red marker post on it and appears to have a reasonable surface but it soon becomes uneven and narrow and no longer accessible for wheels, so from the picnic site retrace your route back to Forest Lodge to pick up the rest of the walk. From Forest Lodge continue until the main path bears right and a path with a white and blue trail marker post goes to the left. Take this path to the left and you are now on the white Dormouse trail. This part may be muddy in winter or after rain. Continue on this trail past another white and blue marker post. Keep ahead when the blue trail goes off to the left. The path shortly curves right to meet a main ride through the woods, where you should turn right. This is a good place to see glow-worms on summer evenings. Continue on this ride, which takes you back to the entrance and the end of the walk.

Henlow and Henlow Park

Accessibility grading ⊛⊛

Reasonably easy terrain throughout, with hard or firm earth surfaces all the way. Some surfaces are uneven and some may be muddy after rain or in winter.

Distance

A circular walk with a couple of spurs, about 2 ½ miles in total. The walk is covered by Ordnance Survey Explorer map 193.

Directions and Parking

The village of Henlow is situated on the A6001 just north of its junction with the A507. It is usually possible to park near the church, but take care not to obstruct the entrance. The church is in the road opposite the Five Bells pub.

Refreshments and Facilities

There are several pubs in the village that serve food and drink. The Five Bells is nearest to the start of the walk and has wheelchair access, including a suitable toilet.

Points of Interest

The walk takes in Henlow Park and Grange and part of the village itself with its interesting mix of properties. There are many large Horse Chestnut and Beech trees in the park and wildflowers in the spring. You are likely to see a variety of birds and may even see a black squirrel, a variant of the grey squirrel, in which the black pigment dominates. They are very rare in most of Britain, but found more frequently in Bedfordshire and surrounding counties. It is thought they may be descendants of black squirrels introduced at Woburn Abbey.

Henlow is an attractive village surrounded by farmland, which is mentioned in the Doomsday Book. Several interesting old buildings remain, including the Maltings, two old school buildings and the Crown pub. The Church itself dates from the 13th century.

The **Village pump** was built in 1897 in celebration of Queen Victoria's 60 years on the throne. It was restored in 1977 to commemorate Queen Elizabeth II's Silver Jubilee.

The **Village sign**, which is near the pump, is a newer addition, being commissioned in 1993 by the Parish Council.

Henlow Grange has been well known for many years as a health farm, and is used by many famous people from the worlds of television, cinema and sport. However, it is a fine Grade II listed Georgian building, and the old house with its clock tower and gates can be clearly distinguished from later extensions. It has been home to many important and famous people over the years, including Lord Boyd of Merton, who granted independence to many former British Colonies when he was Colonial Secretary. The Boyd Memorial Scout Field, near the church, was presented by him.

THE WALK

Two spurs have been included to lengthen and enhance the walk. They are both attractive sections but on both you will have to retrace your route as the path becomes inaccessible. You can miss either or both of these out if you prefer a shorter walk.

From the church continue down the road away from the village, passing through the entrance to the grounds of Henlow Middle School. Go through the opening at the side of a gate onto a track, which continues in the same direction and heads towards Henlow Grange. After a short while there is a track to the left, which you should take to do the first spur. If you want to omit this spur, go straight to Main walk continued below.

First Spur

This spur goes down past the side of Henlow Grange, so look out for celebrities who often visit the health farm here! When you come to

Village pump

a bridge over the river, cross it and follow the path, as it turns left. This takes you along past lakes, which are former gravel workings and are now a habitat for water birds. However, this is private land and it is only possible to glimpse the lakes through the trees. Eventually you come to a private car park belonging to an angling association and at this point the path becomes less accessible, so you should retrace your steps back over the bridge towards the path you left earlier. Turn left to rejoin the original path. Henlow Grange is on your left.

Main walk continued

Continue towards Henlow Grange. In front of the Grange there is a path to the right, which takes you back to the village. If you want to do the second spur, go to Second Spur. If not, turn right and go to Return to Village.

Second Spur

Continue ahead and go past the Grange and through a gap at the side of a gate across the path. Shortly after, there is a second gate across the path, where you can go through the gate at the side. Go ahead here, not left on to a footpath. Soon you will be going through an attractive avenue of trees down to the A507. Look out for black squirrels, which are often seen here. When you reach the A507 you will need to retrace your steps back to Henlow Grange and go left opposite it towards the village.

Return to Village

After a while, the road bears right into Park Lane. You should take this road but make sure you see the amazing topiary in the garden of the old gatehouse as the road goes to the right. Continue along Park Lane past the recreation ground, village hall and lower school. This is a pleasant village street and the properties are an interesting mix of old and new. At the end of Park Lane, turn right to get back to the church.

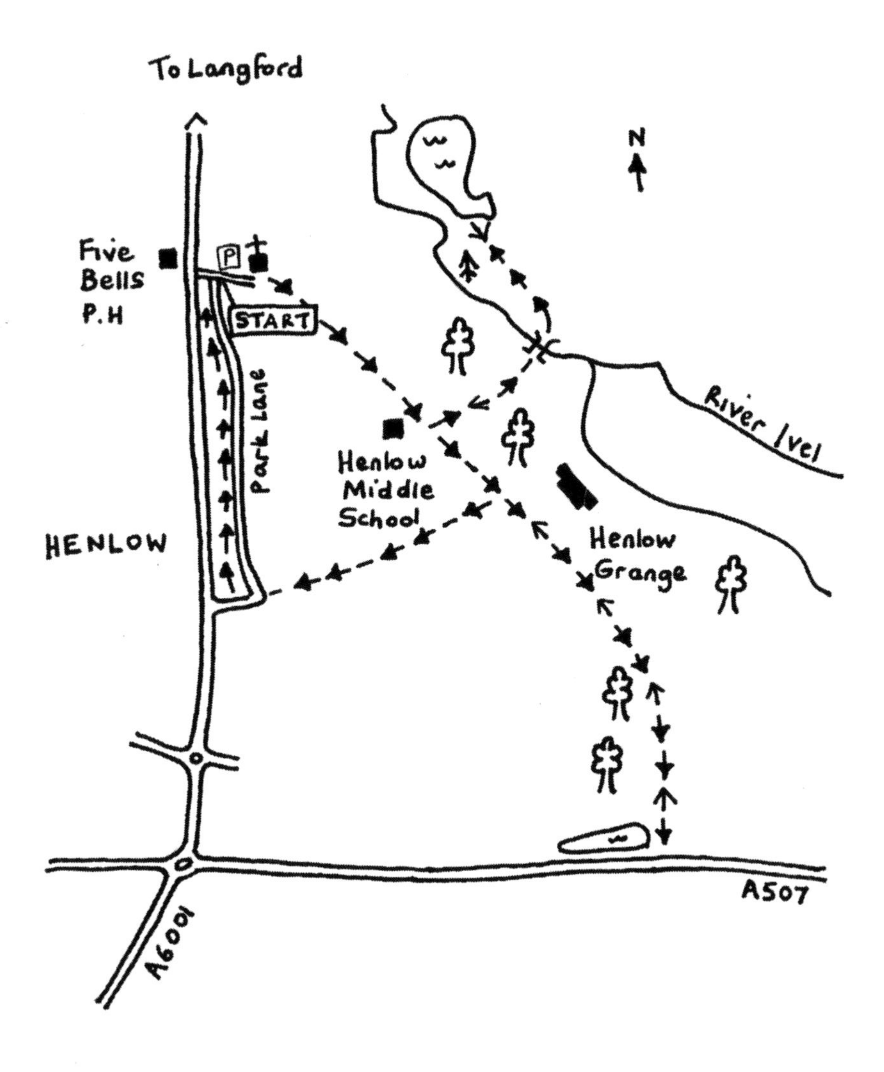
To Langford
N
Five Bells P.H
P
START
Park Lane
Henlow Middle School
River Ivel
Henlow Grange
HENLOW
A507
A6001

Arlesey Mill Pits

Accessibility grading 

This route is on easy terrain throughout, on hard tracks most of the way with a short distance on a flat grassy surface. The route has been graded 2 wheels because Mill Lane is quite steep. The kissing gates are wheelchair-friendly and can also be opened with a radar key if required.

Distance

From the village hall to the weir and back is about 2 miles. The route is covered by the Ordnance Survey Explorer map 193.

Directions and Parking

Arlesey is a long village, which runs south from the A507. It is signposted at the roundabout shortly after crossing the railway on Arlesey Bridge if coming from the west. Turn first left after leaving the roundabout and left again at a T-junction to go through the village. The walk starts from the Village Hall car park, which is on the left hand side, just past the Gothic Mede Lower School.

Alternatively, for a shorter walk or to avoid Mill Lane, there are two disabled parking places at the far end of Mill Lane, courtesy of the landowners, just before the riverside path.

Note that using Mill Lane on a weekday is not currently recommended for wheelchair and mobility scooter users because many large vehicles use the road. On weekdays you should therefore use the alternative parking at the end of Mill Lane.

Refreshments and Facilities

There are several pubs in the village for food and drink, including The Three Tuns near the start point of the route.

Points of Interest

The walk goes through the village of Arlesey and incorporates an easy access path along the banks of the River Hiz, which hosts a variety of wildlife.

The route was devised by Arlesey Conservation for Nature (ACORN) as a partner in the Bedfordshire County Council P3. It is one of a series of local walks, another one of which is currently being made accessible to all users. Further details are available on the website www.arleseywalks.co.uk

Outside the village hall, you can see a replica of the **village pump**. The original once stood at the junction where the road splits into three, as described in the walk details section.

There were originally three mills in Arlesey, all mentioned in the Doomsday Book. One of these was situated at the bridge and weir at the end of the route, and you can still see the remains of the millrace in the water here.

On the right hand side of the road soon after the start, you will see an old granary. It is an 18th-century Grade 2 listed building, previously in the grounds of Moorlands Farmhouse, which was built in 1880.

THE WALK

Turn left on leaving the car park and continue through the village for about a quarter of a mile. Notice the old granary on the opposite side of the road. Continue past the Methodist Church then take the road going to the right, which immediately splits into three roads. Take the middle of the three, Mill Lane, which climbs quite steeply and goes over the railway bridge. A footway is provided on the left side but, because of access restrictions, wheelchair and mobilility scooter users should keep to the right side of the road, being watchful of oncoming traffic and using the footway provided on the bridge section. Once over the bridge, turn right, being aware of traffic coming from the left. This is still Mill Lane and you should follow it down and left to its end. There are two disabled parking spaces here, courtesy of the landowners, if you prefer just a short

Arlesey Mill Pits

walk or perhaps to get into the country for a picnic or to watch nature.

Go along the path and through a kissing gate. Continue along the path, which runs beside the river and alongside a conifer nursery. The hard surface ends as you come to another kissing gate but the surface beyond is firm and grassy and should be accessible at most times of the year. Go through the gate into the water meadows, where cattle may be grazing. This is the most attractive part of the walk and you may see various birds and waterfowl alongside and in the water. If you are very lucky you may even see a kingfisher.

Eventually you come to a weir and a bridge crossing the river.

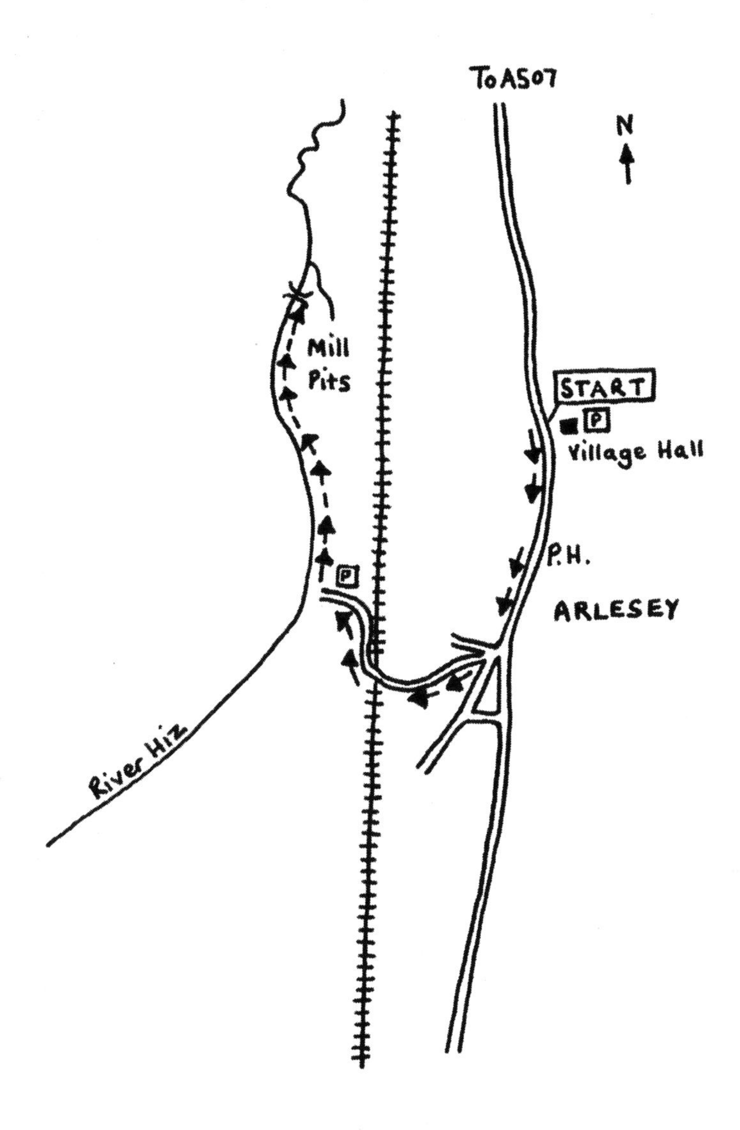

This is a pretty spot and a good place for a picnic. There is also a bridge over to your right but unfortunately the path beyond both these bridges is not very accessible, so you should retrace your steps to the start of the walk.

Woburn and the Abbey

Accessibility grading ⊛⊛⊛⊛ or ⊛⊛

The four-wheel graded route is mainly on grassy or firm surfaced footpaths, some of which may be stony or rutted and may be muddy in winter or after a spell of bad weather. There are also some inclines.

An alternative, graded two wheels, uses the roads within the Abbey grounds. To do this you will need to buy a pass at the ticket office and drive round the roads to the Abbey car park. Unfortunately, this cannot be a circular route from Woburn as a section of the road has been closed except to vehicles for health and safety reasons. The roads pass through a very attractive part of the Deer Reserve but are fairly steep in parts. You may wish to avoid weekends if using this route, especially in the summer, as people visiting the Abbey by car also use these roads.

Distance

The four-wheel graded route from the car park opposite the church in Woburn to the Abbey and back is about 3 miles. The two-wheel graded route from the Abbey car park to Chambers Bridge and back is about 3½ miles, but you could retrace your steps at any point.

Directions and Parking

Woburn lies on the A4012 between the M1 and the A5.

For the four-wheel graded route park in the free car park opposite Woburn Church, which is reached by turning left in the centre of the town when coming from the Bedford direction.

Refreshments and Facilities

There are refreshments available in the Abbey complex, which you can use if you have bought a pass at the ticket office on the route, and in the various pubs and restaurants in the town itself. There are toilets, including disabled access ones, by the Abbey Car Park and these are available to everyone.

Some of the many deer living in the Park

Points of Interest

Woburn Abbey is well known as the home of the Dukes of Bedford. It was built on the site of a Cistercian Monastery dating back to 1145 and is surrounded by a Deer Park covering 3,000 acres, which was landscaped by Humphrey Repton. Over a thousand deer live here and you are certain to see groups of them during your visit. There are nine different species in the Park, ranging from the tiny Muntjac, which have colonised the whole of southern England through escaping from Woburn, to Pere David's deer, introduced in 1894 from the Imperial Herd of China, thus saving the breed from extinction.

THE WALK

Two-wheel graded route

Drive to the Abbey car park following the signs from Woburn past the church. Once parked, you can retrace the route you came in on round the Abbey grounds, as far as Chambers Bridge, then back to the car park.

Four-wheel graded route

Turn right out of Woburn car park and go along the pavement towards the entrance to the Abbey grounds. The pavement is a bit uneven in places so care is needed. At the Abbey entrance there is a narrow high gate on the right-hand side of the road. If this is too narrow for you to pass, cross the road, go through the rightmost of the two gates there, and cross back again. A grassy bank and posts may make this a bit difficult.

Take the footpath, a flat surfaced path, which bears right into parkland, with mature trees and a lake on the left, showing reflections of the trees in the water. After a while, the path joins a small road, which goes past some pretty cottages before entering the park over a cattle grid. Use the gate to the left of the cattle grid and follow the road which bears left and immediately right on to a wide road going between a group of park buildings and stables on the right and a half-timbered building on the left.

You will then come to the ticket office for visiting the Abbey. If you are only using the public footpaths you don't have to pay, but you may like to explain this to the person manning the office. If you want to use the Deer Park roads or go into the Abbey complex you will need to get a pass from the ticket office. Follow the road past Horse Pond and soon the road bears left and a signposted footpath continues ahead. From this point the road is out of bounds except for vehicles.

Continue ahead on the signposted footpath, which is flat and mainly grassy but stony in places. It can also be muddy here after rain. The path goes alongside the Shoulder of Mutton pond, which

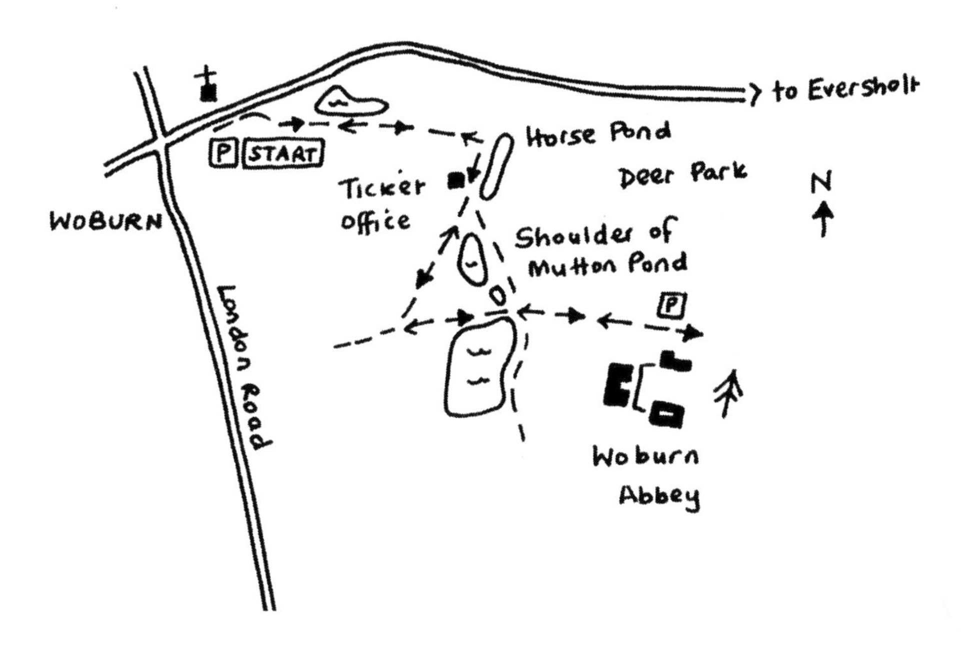

usually has lots of wildfowl. Continue until you see a sign over to the right by a high gate showing a junction of footpaths. Turn left here on to a footpath heading directly towards the Abbey. This is part of the Greensand Ridge Walk, Bedfordshire's first long-distance footpath, which follows the ridge for 40 miles between Leighton Buzzard and Gamlingay and is indicated by a symbol of a muntjac deer.

The path here is all grassy and climbs slightly. You pass a lake on your right, then cross a park road and continue, again climbing steadily. The Abbey is ahead to your right. Finally the footpath reaches the Abbey itself, with car parking, picnic area and toilets. Using the public footpaths only, you will not be able to go any further, so you will need to retrace your route back to the car park, but this is no great hardship as the views over the parkland are so lovely that it is good to see them from a different direction.

Leaving the Abbey, pick up the footpath ahead, which is signposted from the Car Park, not the road that bears right. Follow

Woburn Abbey

the footpath as it goes ahead over the grass, not the road going left. There are beautiful views of the lakes from this vantage point above them. Staying on the footpath, follow the yellow markers downhill and, where the footpath turns right, follow this to retrace your steps to the car park. Take care when going back from the ticket office to go ahead to the gate next to the cattle grid; do not follow the road to the right. Also ensure that after the cottages, you go ahead on the path; do not take the road that curves to the right here.

Stockgrove Country Park

Accessibility grading ⊛ or ⊛⊛⊛

The path around the lake is designated an Easy Access Route, suitable for wheelchairs and pushchairs. It is on flat hard or compacted earth surfaces all the way and is graded one wheel.

Other suggestions for more challenging extensions to the walk are graded 3 wheels.

This route could be muddy in winter or after heavy rain.

Distance

A circular walk round the lake, with two suggested extensions. Up to 2 miles, depending on the extensions chosen.

Directions and Parking

Stockgrove Country Park is off Brickhill Road, Heath and Reach, near Leighton Buzzard. Follow the brown Country Park signs from the A5 between Little Brickhill and Hockliffe.

There is good parking at the visitor centre, where they ask for a suggested donation of £1. A wheelchair is available to borrow but you should call the ranger's office on 01525 237760 in advance to check availability.

Refreshments

The visitor centre has a café with access via a ramp and there is a picnic area adjacent to the car park. The toilets suitable for disabled people are opened with a radar key.

Points of Interest

Stockgrove Country Park is owned by Bedfordshire and Buckinghamshire County Councils and has been open to the public since 1972. It consists of 80 acres on the Greensand Ridge, an area of lowland heath, which is home to a wide variety of flora and fauna. The country park includes ancient oak woodland, conifer plantations, marshes, meadows, heaths and a lake: a circuit of the lake is the main focus of this walk.

Baker's Wood is a Site of Special Scientific Interest. It is an ancient oak woodland and one of the largest areas of deciduous woodland in Bedfordshire.

The Boathouse on the far side of the lake was built in the late 1920s, which was soon after the lake was dug out. It used to have a thatched roofed folly on the top, which was used as a summerhouse and changing rooms in the days when the lake was used for bathing. Unfortunately this was destroyed by fire in the 1960s but there are plans to build a copy of this building and replace the drawbridge connecting the boathouse to the lake bank.

The Stockgrove Sundial is made from waste sandstone from a nearby quarry, which is millions of years old. There is an information board in front of it explaining how to use it to tell the time. The second extra section takes you to see the sundial.

THE WALK

One- and three-wheel graded route

To pick up the easy access path round the lake, go in front of the visitor centre and ahead on a path which bears left over a boarded section, then turn right. You are on a wide path, with a stream on your right and wooded banks on your left. In spring there are daffodils and primroses along this section, followed later by bluebells, and lots of birds such as Great Tit, Blue Tit, Nuthatch, Tree Creeper and Dunnock, which you may see and hear among the trees and bushes. A board outside the visitor centre tells you which birds have been seen here recently. After a while you pass a bridge on the right. Ignore this and the path to the left and continue ahead. Baker's Wood rises on your left and the lake is now on your right. Here you can see waterfowl, such as mallard, coot, moorhen and the brightly coloured Mandarin Duck, originally introduced to this country from eastern Asia. The female lays her eggs in down-filled

The Boathouse

holes in trees, so if you are in the park in springtime, you may be lucky enough to spot a nest hole.

Continue alongside the lake, past a long bench on the left of the path with open views over the water towards the Boathouse. You will pass another bench and then reach the end of the lake. Ignore the path going ahead here and cross the bridge, then turn right to go along the other side of the lake. There are more seats spaced around the water at regular intervals, which make good spots to stop and enjoy the view. Soon you will come to the Boathouse, which has an information board explaining its history. When you come to the end of the lake turn right over the bridge and left to rejoin the path you came in on, retracing your route over the boards to the visitor centre.

The Stockgrove Sundial

Continuation of three-wheel graded route

If you are able to negotiate gentle climbs, there are two extra sections that are well worth including. As you return to the visitor centre on the path after the boarded section, with the centre on your right, take the grassy path that climbs to your left. It is quite narrow and a little uneven in places but has good views and is very pretty especially when the gorse is flowering. There is a seat at the top of the hill, which would be the best place to stop before returning the same way, as there is a steep slope if you continue beyond that.

The second extra section takes you to the Stockgrove sundial. Take the path from the end of the car park nearest the road and furthest from the visitor centre. This is a compacted earth path, which runs parallel to the road initially. It is quite wide and climbs gently to start with, followed by a short steeper section before flattening out on to a wide track. The sundial is just off this wide track. After this the surface is good for a short distance along the ridge but then becomes uneven and hilly, so you will need to return the way you came.

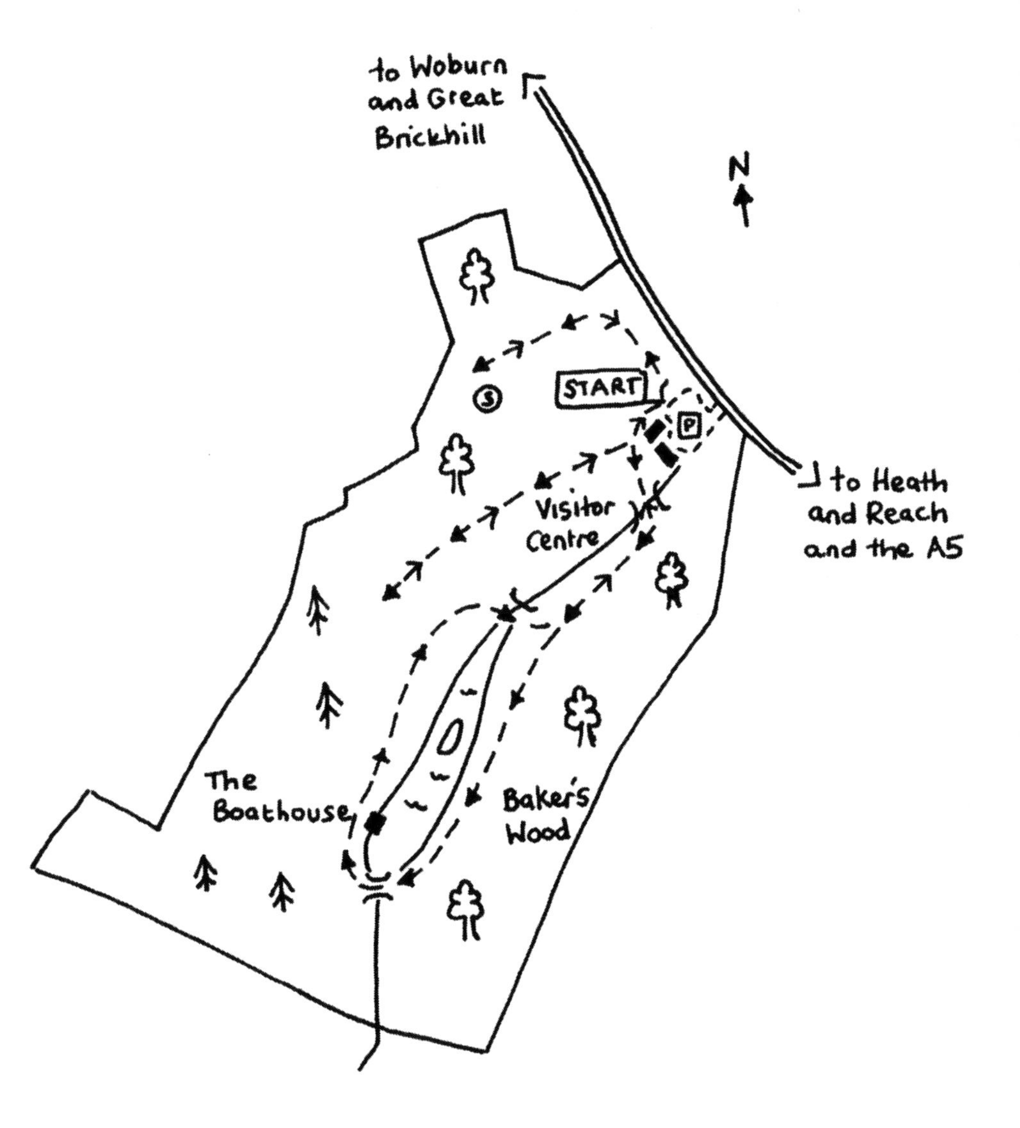

Leighton Buzzard to Bletchley along the Grand Union Canal

Accessibility grading

Easy terrain throughout, on hard flat surfaces most of the way, with some slopes at bridges. The path is generally wide with a firm surface, alongside the water but with a grassy strip separating the path from the canal.

Distance

This is a seven-mile linear route, which offers lots of options for short or long walks as you wish. For example, go as far as one of the pubs for refreshments and return; do the seven miles and arrange transport back; start and/or end at one of the several access points along the route; do the whole route, or just as far as you like, and return. The route is covered by the Ordnance Survey Explorer map 192.

Directions and Parking

The walk is described from Tesco's car park in Leighton Buzzard, where the road crosses the canal (access point 114 on the Grand Union Canal route), up to the car park off Mill Road in the Water Eaton area of Bletchley (access point 98).

There are car parks in Leighton Buzzard and you can park in Tesco's car park for three hours. There is also parking at points along the route, marked on the map.

Refreshments and Facilities

There are two pubs on the route, The Globe and the Three Locks, both of which serve food and have outside tables.

The Globe is a very old building and access to the inside is not very good for wheelchairs. There is a shallow step to get inside from the canal path and there are no wheelchair accessible toilets. The

Bridge over the canal

outside tables, however, are on the route itself.

The Three Locks is also an old building and has a shallow step to the inside from the front and currently no disabled-accessible toilets. It is possible to reach the tables at the rear of the pub with wheels and the best approach is to go past the front, if approaching from the Leighton Buzzard end of the route, and where the path continues alongside the canal, go right to climb a fairly steep ramp past the lock gates.

Refreshments can also be found in Leighton Buzzard and Stoke Hammond near to the route.

Points of Interest

This section of the Grand Union canal towpath has been improved to make it accessible to all. It is part of the National Cycle Network, co-ordinated by Sustrans, the UK's leading sustainable transport society in partnership with Bedfordshire and other County Councils. You can find out more details about Sustrans routes from their website www.nationalcyclenetwork.org.uk.

The route follows the canal all the way and includes several locks, attractive old bridges, waterfowl and waterside pubs where you can sit outside enjoying the setting alongside the canal.

THE WALK

Start the walk at the gap in the fence in Tesco's car park. Turn right to go alongside the canal with the water on your left. This is an attractive spot, with pretty cottages near the water and lots of water birds. There are narrow boats of all colours and sizes moored here, often with unusual and interesting names.

After a short while you will pass the Wyvern Shipping Company, noticeable for the fleet of bright blue boats sometimes moored there, which are hired out for canal holidays. You are very soon out of town and alongside the Ouzel meadows. You pass a set of locks and are truly out in the countryside. Look out for herons on the banks and coot and moorhen on the water. You pass an old swing bridge on the left and a marker saying 'Braunston 45 miles'.

You soon arrive at the Globe pub and restaurant. This is another access point, number 111, with a car park at the pub. There are tables outside near the water and this is a lovely spot for a drink or a meal on a fine day. For accessibility details, see Refreshments and Facilities section.

After the Globe, continue along the canal under the bridge. At this point there are fields on your right. About half a mile further on, there is another access point, number 110, by the bridge taking the road over the canal. Carry on along the footpath, going under

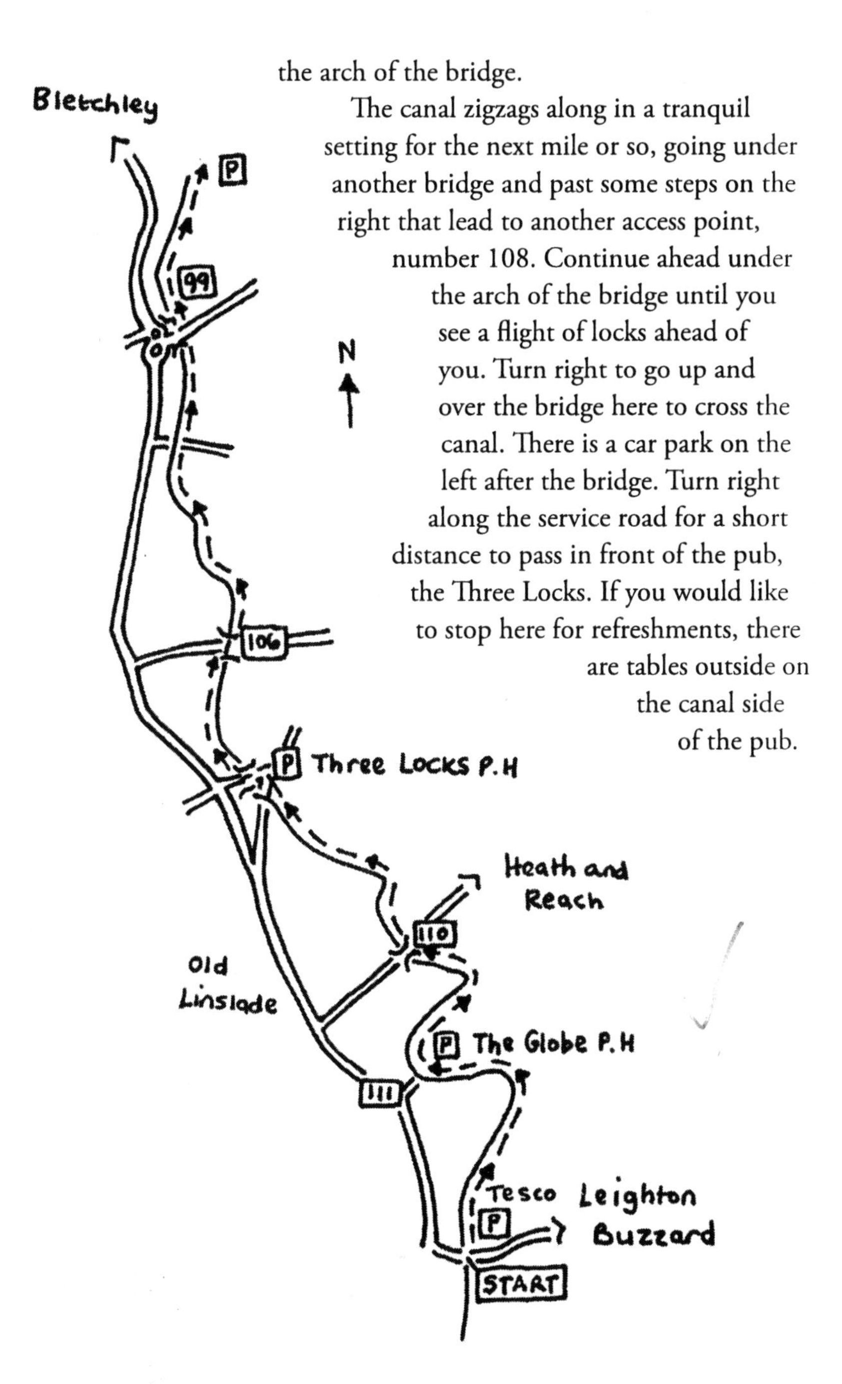

the arch of the bridge.

The canal zigzags along in a tranquil setting for the next mile or so, going under another bridge and past some steps on the right that lead to another access point, number 108. Continue ahead under the arch of the bridge until you see a flight of locks ahead of you. Turn right to go up and over the bridge here to cross the canal. There is a car park on the left after the bridge. Turn right along the service road for a short distance to pass in front of the pub, the Three Locks. If you would like to stop here for refreshments, there are tables outside on the canal side of the pub.

Lock and cottage on the Grand Union Canal

See the Refreshments and Facilities section for accessibility details.

Go past the pub on the service road, then on to the canalside path again, this time with the canal on your right. In about a mile, you come to access point 106 near Stoke Hammond, where you cross the bridge to return to the other side of the canal. Note that the slopes up to and down from the bridge are fairly steep. The water is back on your left again now.

You will shortly pass more locks near Stoke Hammond, go under another bridge and pass a winding hole on the canal, a place for narrow boats to turn round in. After a while, you will see a road close to the canal on the far side, and shortly after that is access point 102, which has steps to get to and from the path. Pass under the bridge with care. You will notice increasing numbers of boats moored here at a marina. At the next bridge, access point 99, instead of going under the arch, go over the bridge and turn on to a wide path running alongside the canal but a little way from it. This is part of the canal broadwalk that runs alongside large sections of the canal in Milton Keynes. Ouzel Valley Waterhall Park is on your right.

When you come to a footpath sign directing you to the riverside walk, you might like to take a short detour on to this walk instead of continuing along the canal broadwalk. To do so turn right past a plantation of cricket bat willows on your right. There is an information board here explaining that when the willows are 20-25 years old they are made into cricket bats of such high quality that they are used by international players. Immediately after the plantation, take the path to the left where the path you are on curves right. Stay on that path and bear right to rejoin the broadwalk along the canal. You will shortly come to half barriers across the path, where you should turn right at the minor road to reach the car park at the end of the route.

Dunstable Downs and Whipsnade Tree Cathedral

Accessibility grading ⊛⊛⊛⊛⊛ or ⊛⊛

Both Dunstable Downs sections of these routes are challenging and the five-wheel graded routes are probably only suitable for pushchairs. Sturdy mobility scooters may be able to negotiate the route but should not attempt it in winter or after heavy rain. Some of the terrain is grassy and uneven, some is on firm but unsurfaced ground and some is on hard surfaces. There are some climbs and parts of the route are very likely to be muddy after rain or in winter.

An alternative route, graded 2 wheels, is to visit Whipsnade Tree Cathedral, parking in the Cathedral Car Park and exploring the plantation.

Distance

The five-wheel route across the Downs and to the Tree Cathedral is a circular walk of about three miles.

The five-wheel route to the Five Knolls Tumuli and back is about 1½ miles in total.

A visit to the Tree Cathedral only will involve an exploration of its 9½ acres, as long or as short a visit as you like.

Directions and Parking

The main car park for Dunstable Downs is off the B4541 out of Dunstable. There is ample parking, including spaces reserved for the disabled. The Tree Cathedral is signposted from the B4540, 1½ miles from Dunstable Downs. This too has good parking.

Refreshments and Facilities

The visitor centre, shop and toilets on Dunstable Downs are all wheelchair accessible, and there is a kiosk serving food and drinks. The centre is open every day from 10am to 5pm from spring to

Mist in the valley from the heights of Dunstable Downs

autumn and weekends only from 10am to 4pm from November to March. The kiosk and toilets are open all year from 10am to dusk, except Christmas Day. A new centre, including an indoor eating area, all of which will be wheelchair-friendly, is due to open in Autumn 2006.

There are no facilities at the Tree Cathedral.

Points of Interest

Dunstable Downs is part of the Chilterns Area of Outstanding Natural Beauty and is designated a Site of Special Scientific Interest (SSSI). It is owned by Bedfordshire County Council, and managed jointly with the National Trust. It is the highest point in Bedfordshire, approximately 800 feet above sea level, and offers fine views over the Chilterns and the Vale of Aylesbury.

The chalk grasslands are home to a wide variety of plants and

Whipsnade Tree Cathedral

wildlife, including some uncommon species of plants and butterflies. Because chalk is difficult to cultivate, the Downs were mainly used over the centuries for grazing sheep, and this has created the chalk grasslands we have today. Since World War II there has been a decline in sheep grazing, but this has now been reintroduced in order to preserve this rare habitat.

In addition, the Downs are a popular spot for kite flying, gliding and paragliding.

The Pillow Mounds are thought to be the site of a medieval rabbit warren, where the animals were bred for their meat and skins.

Five Knolls is the site of a Round Barrow Cemetery, the only known site in Bedfordshire. A barrow is an individual burial mound, with later burials dug into the sides.

The Tree Cathedral on the edge of Whipsnade Village Green is owned by the National Trust and was created after the First World War in a spirit of 'Faith, hope and reconciliation'. It is mainly intended as a place of worship, meditation and quiet enjoyment of nature. The plantation contains many different tree species laid out in the form of a cathedral. Grass avenues form the chancel, nave, transepts, four chapels and cloisters in an area covering nine and a half acres.

THE WALKS

Five-wheel graded walks

Walks 1 and 2, both graded five wheels for accessibility, start from the visitor centre.

Two-wheel graded walk

An alternative walk, graded two wheels for accessibility, starts from the Tree Cathedral car park (see Directions and Parking section). There are no further details for this walk as the plantation can be explored whichever way you prefer.

Five-wheel graded walk 1
The Downs and Tree Cathedral

Leave the main car park by the disabled spaces and turn left over the grass, going past the car park and climbing slightly. The grass can be quite long and rough here but the surface improves in a short while. Go along the ridge, heading towards the trees in the distance. This is a popular kite-flying area. Veer to the right heading towards a path between trees. This is the Icknield Way bridleway. The path is wide but can be uneven. Go through a gate – you may need to reach through to open the latch, as with many of the gates on the Downs, but they open easily – and go ahead. You are now on a wide grassy area, with grazing sheep keeping the grass short. Keep to the grassy well-defined path as the route climbs and then flattens out on top of the ridge. Here you have excellent views over the surrounding countryside, including the Vale of Aylesbury.

Once on the ridge, follow the line of the fence on the right, keeping quite close to it, until you come to a gate. Do not go through this gate, which leads to the Bison Hill car park over rough terrain, but turn left to follow the fence until you reach another gate by a line of trees. Again, do not go through this gate but turn left here and continue round the edge of the field along a wide grassy track, following the fence. After a while, the fence turns right going towards a gate and you should continue to follow it as it does so. Go through the gate on to a bridleway, which continues in the same direction, running alongside the wood. It may be muddy here after rain. Cross a track and continue ahead on the bridleway. Take a right fork and pass Evergreen Lodge on the left. At this point there are woods on both sides of the path, which now has a hard surface and remains so until almost the Tree Cathedral. Ignore a footpath sign to the right and a bridleway sign to the left and continue along this quiet tree lined road. There are signs indicating Sallowsprings nature reserve on the left.

Take the next bridleway to the right, at a National Trust sign, to bring you to the Tree Cathedral. There is a kissing gate here, which gives access to the tree cathedral but it is more accessible to turn left at the kissing gate and follow the bridleway for a short distance until it comes out by the car park. You can enter the Tree Cathedral from the car park through a kissing gate, which is suitable for wheeled access, including mobility scooters. The paths within the cathedral are mainly on short grass, and all are flat.

After your visit, retrace your steps by going left out of the car park on to the bridleway and following the bridleway and path back the way you came until you come out on to the downs.

Turn right and you will soon come to a gate, after which the path is fairly narrow but leads back over the downs to the Visitor Centre and Car Park. If this path looks unsuitable, turn left before the gate and right through the gate you used on the outward route. Go back over the downs to the Car Park.

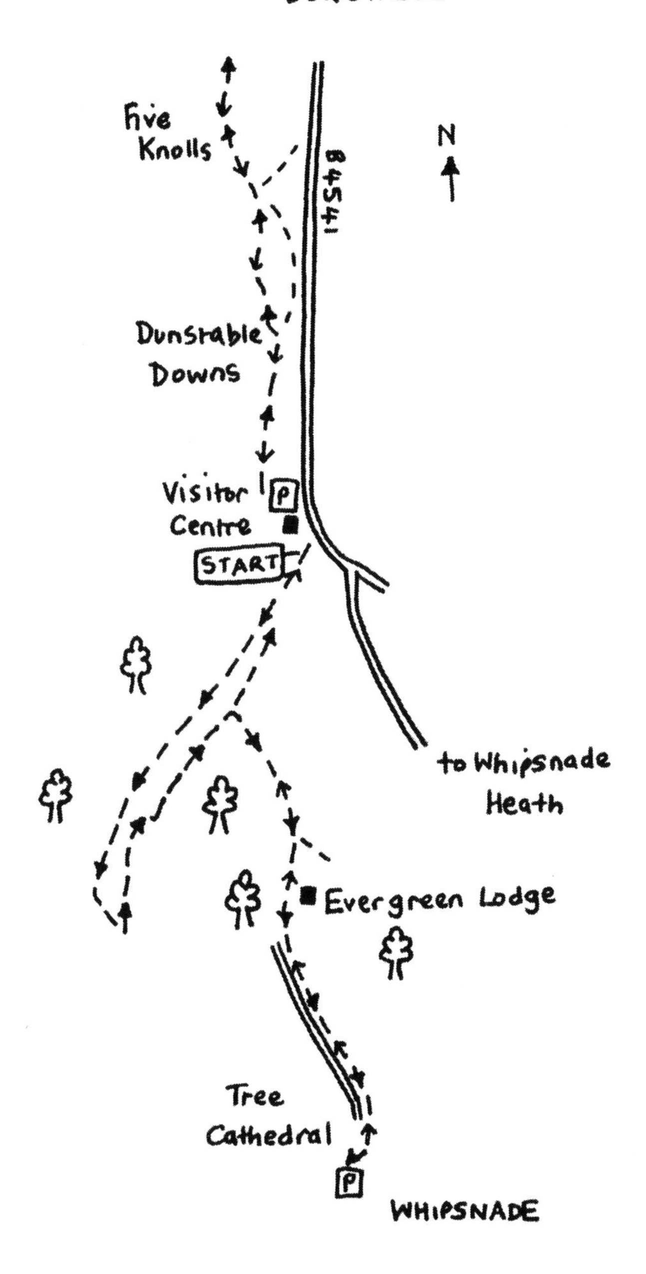
DUNSTABLE
Five Knolls
B4541
N
Dunstable Downs
Visitor Centre
P
START
to Whipsnade Heath
Evergreen Lodge
Tree Cathedral
P
WHIPSNADE

Five-wheel graded walk 2
Five Knolls Tumuli and Pillow Mounds

Leave the car park on a surfaced path going past some benches, and continuing on grass past more benches. Go between the wooden posts and on to a chalky track, which can be quite soft after rain. Go through a car parking area and veer left on to a wide grassy path, rather than taking the higher route, which is nearer the road. As you continue ahead, you will see Five Knolls in front of you and will have spectacular views from this point on. There is a track ahead but to get to it there is a short, fairly narrow and awkward section, which you will need to negotiate with care. This track too can be soft and slippery after rain. There are two gates ahead, a kissing gate on the left and fully opening gate on the right, higher up. You will need to have a good head for heights here. The views are superb, and the paths are wide, but there is a drop on the left. At a fork of footpaths, take the left one to go over the little hill and down the other side, following the footpath sign. You are now in the Pillow Mounds, a very attractive area, on a path between the grassy mounds. At the end of the path on Five Knolls, you have good views over Dunstable and the surrounding countryside.

Retrace your steps to return to the Visitor Centre and car park.

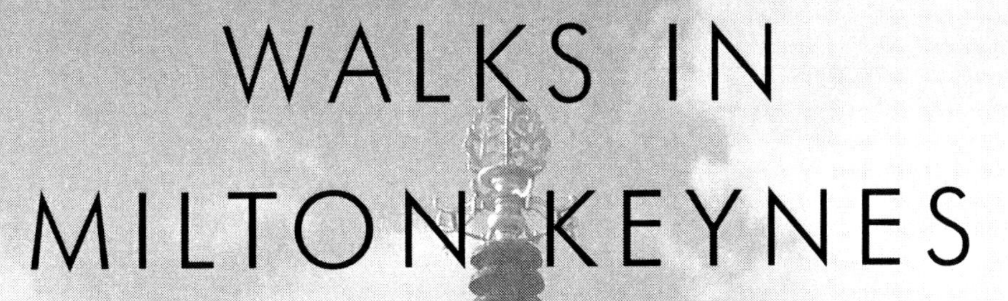
WALKS IN
MILTON KEYNES

Campbell Park and Grand Union Canal

Accessibility grading 

Easy terrain throughout, using Redways and Leisure routes and on hard flat surfaces all the way.

There are several cattle grids in Campbell Park, but they all have a wide kissing gate suitable for wheelchair access at the side.

Distance

A circular walk of about 4 miles.

Directions and Parking

Campbell Park lies between Portway H5 and Childs Way H6 to the east of Marlborough Street V8. The walk starts from the canal side car park, reached by going south from the North Overgate roundabout, and left at the Cricket Green roundabout. Note that there is a height barrier at the entrance of 6'3" (1.90m). The car park is alongside the canal, where colourful narrow boats are often moored.

Refreshments and Facilities

There is a café on the route, Camphill Café, which serves snacks and light lunches. There is a ramp to the inside and the garden tables are all accessible, but they do not currently have a toilet suitable for disabled access.

Points of Interest

The route is divided between the canal side and parkland, so is very varied. As well as exploring Campbell Park, it takes in part of the Canal Broadwalk, which is a firm wide path, running alongside the Grand Union Canal for some three and a half miles.

Campbell Park is the premier park in Milton Keynes and hosts many festivals and other events. It has formal gardens, which are attractive all year round, woodland areas that are spectacular in

Chain Reaction statue

autumn and good for picking blackberries, sculptures and lots of activities from cricket to kite flying.

The Labyrinth is found at the top end of the park and is an outdoor puzzle with a working sundial at its centre, created by local artist Justin Tunley.

Chain Reaction is a very distinctive and striking sculpture by Ray Smith. It is a column of figures linked together and was designed to be viewed from all angles.

The City Gardens run along the whole northern edge of the park and are full of ornamental shrubs so that there is colour and interest all year round. It also has a series of streams and ponds ending in a lily pond overlooking the cricket green.

The **Cricket Ground** is maintained to a high standard and hosts a full programme of matches of all standards, so if you are visiting the park in the summer months, you are very likely to be able to see a game.

THE WALK

Go left alongside the canal and you will soon pass under Portway H5. Look out for water birds and listen to the birds singing in the trees and bushes lining the route. The path soon curves past a recreation area and a bridge on the right over the canal, which you should ignore. Carry on ahead, ignoring a second bridge over the canal. You will pass some paddocks on your left and go under Dansteed Way H4. At this point the path curves to the left, and you should then take the right fork over a bridge at Skeats Wharf. There are some attractive houses here with moorings on the water.

Soon the path curves left and there is a bridge on the right over the canal. Cross the bridge and turn right to go back towards Campbell Park down the other side of the canal. Head back towards Dansteed Way H4 down a pleasant poplar-lined route. This is part of the canal broadwalk, large sections of which are lined with poplars. Shortly after passing under H4, there is a bridge over the canal, which you should ignore. You then pass a playground on your left where the path bears slightly away from the canal. Take the broadwalk here to the right and follow it round until it brings you to a playground, then carry straight on to the canal and a footpath crossroads.

Go straight ahead here to continue alongside the canal, unless you wish to visit the Camphill Café (see the Refreshments section).

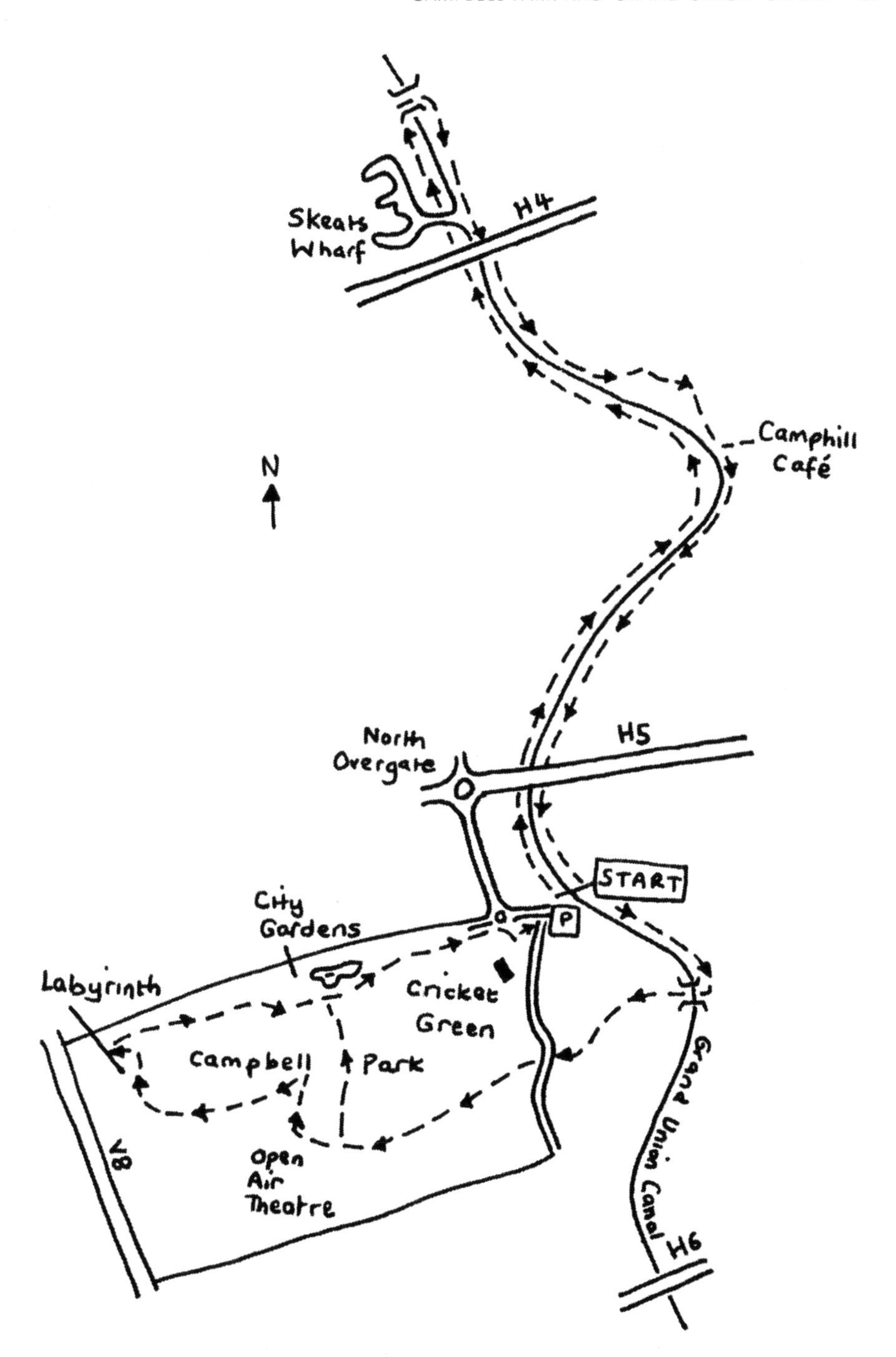
H4
Skeats Wharf
Camphill Café
N
North Overgate
H5
START
City Gardens
P
Labyrinth
Cricket Green
Campbell Park
Open Air Theatre
V8
Grand Union Canal
H6

Narrowboat moored on Grand Union Canal

If so, go left at this crossroads away from the canal for about 50 metres. Return to the canal side after your visit and turn left to continue your route with the water on your right.

Pass under Portway H5, and continue until you reach a crossroads signposted to Campbell Park. Cross the bridge here into the park and go ahead, away from the canal, passing the metal sculpture of a head. There are lots of benches here and it is a pleasant spot for a break or a picnic. Look out too for birds, such as green woodpeckers. Keep going ahead – the path climbs slightly here – until there is a fork in the path, with a bridge on the right fork. Take this bridge over a road and continue ahead on the path through the middle of the park, which is route 51. You will see the cricket green and pavilion on the right. Continue ahead at the junction of footpaths. Go straight ahead through a metal kissing gate. There are sometimes sheep in this field. Ignore any paths to the left and continue ahead until you reach a crossroads, which has a tree with a seat around it in the middle. Here you will see a viewpoint above you and the path which curves round to it, climbing gently. This climb and the subsequent slopes behind the Labyrinth can be avoided if necessary by turning right here and rejoining the walk by the Chain Reaction statue.

The path to the viewpoint curves past the Open-air Theatre until it reaches the top of the hill, from where there are good views over Milton Keynes. After admiring the views, do not descend the way you came, but take the other path through a gate next to a cattle grid and follow it as it curves right towards the Labyrinth, an interesting place to stop. Take the path out of the back of the Labyrinth and pick up a path going right. There are some fairly steep slopes down in this section. Go through another metal kissing gate and you will soon come to the Chain Reaction statue and should continue ahead. If you have avoided the viewpoint, you will rejoin the walk by the statue and turn right.

On your left now are the City Gardens, with gates taking you to paths running through them. Go through the third gate, over the bridge and turn right to follow the path over another bridge, under a pagoda and past duck ponds with seats by them.

At a T-junction, turn right over a small bridge and turn left to rejoin the main path. You will see the cricket pavilion ahead. Follow the path as it curves round the left of the pavilion, cross the road leading to the pavilion car park and you will see ahead of you the canal side car park where you started the walk.

Willen Lake

Accessibility grading 

Easy terrain throughout, with hard flat surfaces most of the way. There are a couple of short climbs.

Distance

This is a circular walk just under 3 miles using Milton Keynes' Redways and Leisure routes.

Directions and Parking

Willen Lake is on the eastern edge of Milton Keynes, bordered on the south by Childs Way H6 and on the west and east by Brickhill Street V10 and Tongwell Street V11. Go north from the H6 at the Woolstone roundabout and right at the Newlands roundabout to get to the Newlands car park on the South Lake, where there is ample parking, including bays for disabled badge holders.

Refreshments and Facilities

By the lakeside and to the right of the start point of the walk, beyond the cycle hire building there is a kiosk selling drinks, snacks and ice creams. There are toilets here too, including one with disabled access. A little further along in the same direction is a pub and restaurant, which have good access, including disabled access toilets. The route passes these at the end of the walk.

Points of Interest

Willen Lake was built in the 1970s and now gets over a million visitors a year. It comprises two lakes: a bustling South Lake where a variety of water sports and activities take place and a quieter North Lake. The route described goes round both lakes in a clockwise direction. It is very varied and takes you past a number of interesting landmarks as well as giving you the opportunity to see Willen's rich birdlife.

Peace Pagoda

The Peace Pagoda is a famous Milton Keynes landmark. It was the first peace pagoda to be built in Europe and houses sacred relics of the Lord Buddha. The outside has a series of spectacular carvings, which tell a story. This symbol of peace and brotherhood was built and is maintained by monks and nuns who live in the nearby Buddhist temple and who hold an annual open-air festival of music, song and prayer to celebrate its anniversary.

The Circle of Hearts Medicine Wheel is another peace symbol you will pass on the walk. It was built by people from Milton Keynes to welcome the new millennium and is a symbol of peace and harmony. An interpretation board gives a full explanation of its meaning.

Willen Village. The name Willen probably meant 'at the willows', a reference to the trees along the banks of the river Ouzel. There has been a village on this site for many years, but during the

17th-century church of St Mary Magdalene

last few centuries it has never had a population of more than 100 people. The seventeenth-century church of St Mary Magdalene with its ornate tower is very striking. It was designed by Robert Hooke, a schoolfellow of Sir Christopher Wren.

Birds. North Willen Lake attracts birdwatchers from across Britain who come to enjoy the huge variety of species that live in or visit the park, some of which are rare. Identification panels around the lake help you to spot the different species. The lake has been continuously improved to provide habitats to attract birds and the island is an ideal sanctuary for nesting birds, including ducks, geese and other water birds not usually seen in towns, such as Redshank and Common Tern. The bird population swells in winter when immigrant waterfowl arrive, and in spring and autumn during the migration period you may see rare species, such as the Osprey which visited the lake on its way south.

View over North Lake

THE WALK

Go down to the water and turn left. You will keep the water on your right all through the walk. You will soon reach the end of South Lake, where there is a path to the right going round this lake. Ignore this path and go straight ahead, passing under the road, and continuing ahead towards North Lake. On your right you pass the Circle of Hearts Medicine Wheel, and just after this, take the compacted gravel surface, a Greenway, which forks right from the path you are on. This path is nearer to the water than the Redway that runs alongside it and eventually continues round the top of the lake, which the Redway does not.

The next landmark is the Peace Pagoda on your left, which can be seen between the bushes from the path you are on.

The lake here is fringed with bulrushes and attracts many wading birds and wildfowl at various times of the year, including Curlew,

Oystercatcher, Black-tailed Godwit, Mandarin duck, Great-crested Grebe and Goldeneye.

Keep to the path following the edge of the lake, which now goes through a more wooded area before passing Willen Hospice and skirting Willen Village. The 17th-century church of St Mary Magdalene is behind the Hospice.

After Willen village, bear right to keep close to the lake, passing on your left first the archaeological site of Willen Mill and then the Flood Control Structure. Taking up floodwater from the river was one of the reasons for building the lake. There are a couple of short climbs on this stretch.

When you see the path going under Portway H5 ahead, you have the option of a short extra section to visit the bird hide. This is an accessible open structure offering good views over the water with the chance to spot many varieties of birds.

If you would like to do this, before going under the road, go down to the water's edge, turn right to go over the bridge and follow the signs to the hide, about 200m away. After visiting the hide, retrace your route to the point just before the path goes under the road.

Go under the road and continue ahead, now with South Lake on your right. This is a straight section right by the water, with few trees or bushes to obstruct the view.

Turn right at the end of the lake, keeping to the path near the water, which then joins another trail bearing right. You will pass part of the miniature railway track on your left and then the lakeside pub and restaurant, which is accessible for wheels and has a disabled access toilet. Notice the bird feeding areas, designed to limit the damage caused by indiscriminate feeding. Soon you will pass a kiosk selling drinks and snacks, where there are more toilets including a disabled access one. The car park is on the left just after the information board.

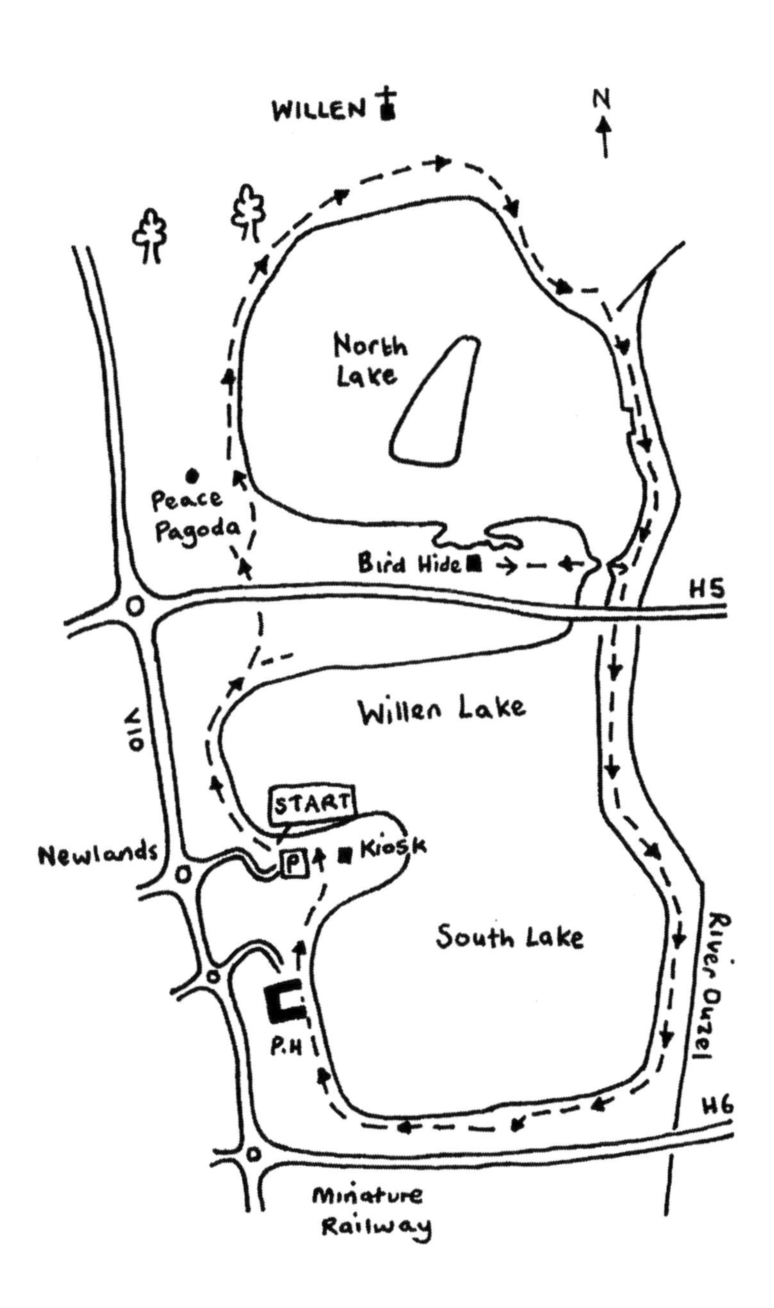
WILLEN
N
North Lake
Peace Pagoda
Bird Hide
H5
Willen Lake
V10
START
Newlands
P
Kiosk
South Lake
River Ouzel
P.H
H6
Miniature Railway

Bradwell Abbey to Loughton Village

Accessibility grading 

Easy terrain throughout, with hard flat surfaces all the way.

Distance

A circular route of about 3 ½ miles.

Directions and Parking

The walk starts from the car park at Bradwell Abbey, which is the first turning on the left when going south from the Stacey Bushes roundabout on H3 Monks Way between the A5 and V6 Grafton Street.

Refreshments and Facilities

There are no refreshments or facilities on this route but there is often a refreshments van parked in the car park at Bradwell Abbey.

Points of Interest

This walk goes from Bradwell Abbey to Loughton Village and includes a 14th-century chapel, a path alongside a brook, Lodge Lake and the attractive green of Loughton Village.

The abbey is not on the walk, but is well worth visiting at the beginning or end by going from the car park towards the cluster of old buildings, where you will find the **City Discovery Centre**. This is a charity set up to promote appreciation of the history and environment, both natural and manmade, of the city of Milton Keynes. It has been based at the heritage site of Bradwell Abbey, which it manages, since 1992.

Bradwell Abbey is the site of a 12th-century Benedictine Priory. Several original buildings remain and have been incorporated into the mainly 17th-century farm buildings. The grounds contain the original medieval fishpond. Turn left along the path in front of the buildings to see the 14th-century chapel of St Mary.

14th-century Chapel of St Mary

Lodge Lake is one of the city's balancing lakes, designed to prevent flooding. It holds excess water and releases it slowly into Loughton brook, thus preventing the flooding of Loughton village, a regular occurrence before the lake was created. The lake is well-known for its fishing and huge carp have been caught here.

Loughton Village originally comprised two villages, separated by the brook, which were joined together to form Loughton Village in 1408. This is a very pretty spot with some of the buildings dating from the sixteenth century.

THE WALK

Start the walk from the path that leads out of the end of the car park nearest the Abbey site, with the cluster of old buildings to the left behind you. It is not signposted but it is a clear path, which leads towards a hedge, where you should turn left on to a wide path. Cross a bridleway and turn right at the signpost indicating 'Lodge Lake'. The path is now following the brook on your left, which sometimes flows rapidly over rocks and sometimes meanders along through the North Loughton Valley Park. After a short while, the path goes under the A5, signposted Lodge Lake and Loughton Village. There is a slight incline up from the underpass. Keep alongside the brook and ignore a path off to the right. Just before the Dansteed Way H4 road bridge, follow the path over a bridge to the other side of the brook and then under the H4.

This brings you out at the northern edge of Lodge Lake. Turn left following the signpost indicating Loughton Village to go round the eastern side of the lake. There are many benches and picnic tables around the water where you might like to stop.

Cross a bridleway and turn right at the car park at the sign to Loughton Village to continue down the side of the lake. This is a very attractive, quiet section, with little inlets, which are good places to see herons or any of the numerous water birds to be found on the lake. At one point the path crosses the lake on a little bridge. Go left at the T-junction, following the sign to Loughton Village, under Portway H5 and ahead, ignoring the path to the left.

Continue with the brook on your left until a fork in the path, where you take the left hand fork to Loughton Village. Go over two bridges where the water rushes over rocks to find yourself with a wider section of water on your right. Cross over a road – you may need to go left to reach a dropped kerb here – and go ahead alongside the brook on your right with houses behind trees on your left. The path turns right on a bridge over the brook to bring you out at the Green in Loughton Village. There is an information board here with interesting details of the village's history and a seat round a tree on the green, which is a pleasant place to stop.

Continue on the path going towards the sports ground and turn right to go round it, passing in front of the pavilion before turning right to the road. Turn right on the path alongside the road and

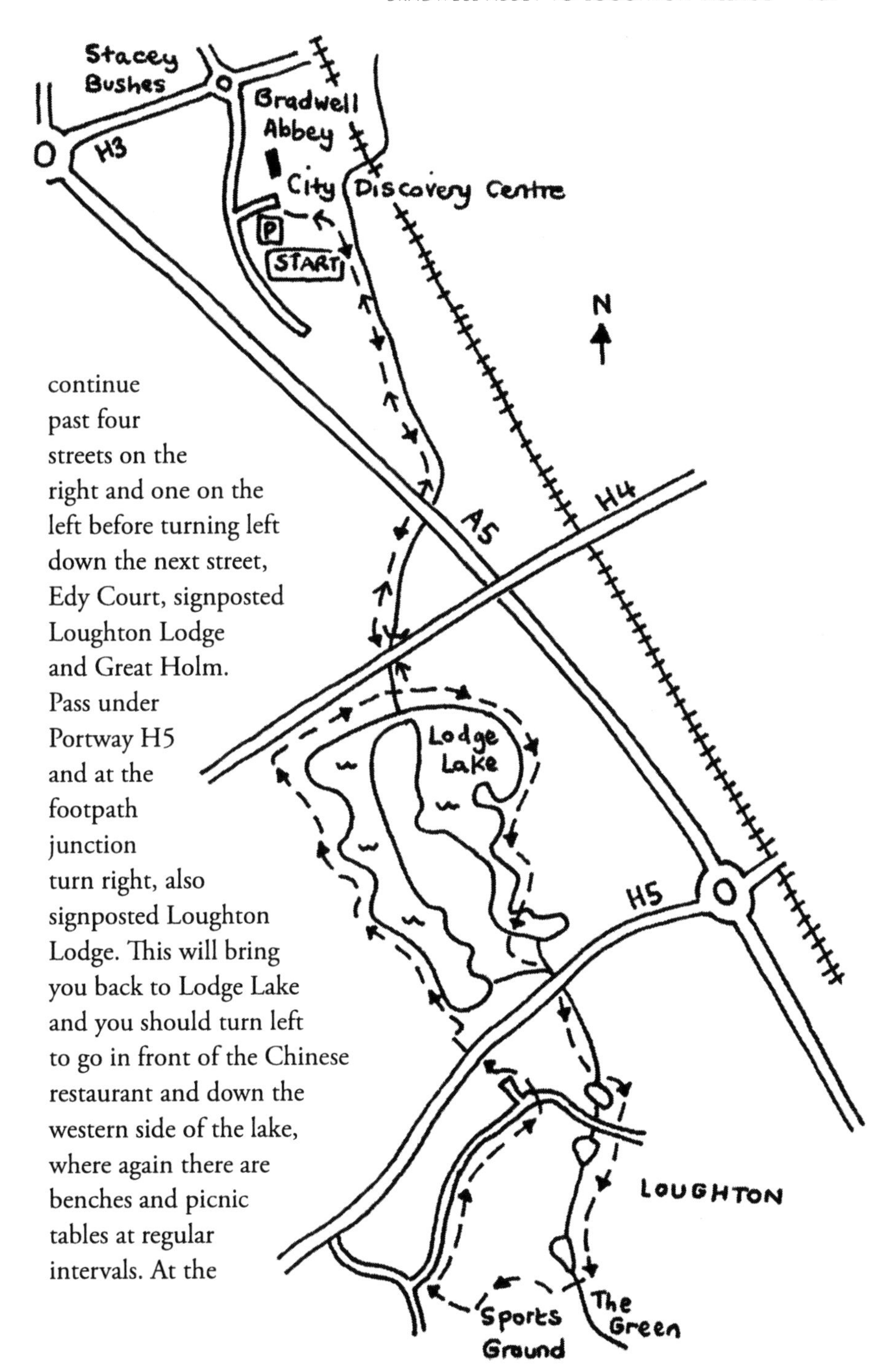

continue past four streets on the right and one on the left before turning left down the next street, Edy Court, signposted Loughton Lodge and Great Holm. Pass under Portway H5 and at the footpath junction turn right, also signposted Loughton Lodge. This will bring you back to Lodge Lake and you should turn left to go in front of the Chinese restaurant and down the western side of the lake, where again there are benches and picnic tables at regular intervals. At the

Loughton village green

end of this side of the lake the path goes away from the water for a short distance, round buildings, then it turns right to go round the northern edge of the lake. Ignore the path that goes off to the left here, signposted Bradwell Abbey. The middle of the lake is a large peninsular with paddocks which at this point is very close to the edge of the lake.

At the next signpost indicating Bradwell Abbey turn left away from the Lake and retrace your outward route from here to the start by going under Dansteed Way H4, over the bridge over the brook and taking the first right running alongside the water. This path takes you back along the brook until you eventually reach a T-junction. Turn left here signposted Bradwell Abbey and look out for the opening in the hedge that leads to the car park.

Ouzel Valley Park

Accessibility grading

Easy terrain throughout, with hard flat surfaces almost all the way. All the gates are wheelchair accessible and there are benches and picnic tables around the park. There are a couple of places that might be muddy after rain.

Distance

A circular walk of about 4½ miles.

Directions and Parking

The walk starts from the car park near the Cricket Green at Woolstone, off Newport road south of H6 Childs Way between Marlborough Street V8 and Brickhill Street V10.

Refreshments and Facilities

The Barge Inn on Newport road in Woolstones Village and the Olde Swan pub in Woughton on the Green are both accessible and have toilets suitable for disabled people.

There are also toilets, including disabled access, a few minutes off the walk on South Willen Lake, which is near the beginning of the route. They are reached by going left instead of right as you reach the lakeside. Retrace your route to rejoin the walk.

Points of Interest

This walk is mainly in the Ouzel Valley Park, which stretches from Walton Lake in the south to Willen Lake in the north. The route is varied and includes lakeside, a poplar plantation, the banks of the River Ouzel, parkland with open views, medieval sites, an orchard where the fruit is free for the taking and the Grand Union Canal.

South Willen Lake is one of the more bustling lakes in Milton Keynes, hosting a variety of water sports. This walk passes along its southern edge.

The poplar plantation lies along the banks of the river Ouzel at the northern end of the park and has a mixture of 19 different species of poplar and some willows, including cricket bat willows, which are used to make cricket bats for international players.

Medieval sites are dotted around the park. They are the remains of villages whose inhabitants may have been wiped out by the great plague in1686 or which were abandoned as their inhabitants moved away from the river to avoid flooding. In the south of the park, you can also see an example of 'ridge and furrow' caused by medieval ploughing, showing that these fields were used for agriculture in medieval times and have not been ploughed since. Look out for the interpretation boards at points of interest.

The community orchard in Woughton on the Green, which you will pass through on the walk, has rows of old English apple trees and all the apples are free to take.

THE WALK

From the car park, turn right and proceed anti-clockwise along the path that curves round Woolstone Sports Ground. You will see some picnic tables over to your right near the site of a medieval moat. If you want to look at this, retrace your route afterwards to continue round the green past houses on the right. At a fork in the path, go right past the pub garden and into Mill Lane, a quiet road leading down past some attractive old houses to a church. Turn right down this lane and cross the road to go in front of and round the church, following the road as it goes past Mill Court House. Turn left on to the redway, heading towards the Woolstone roundabout on H6 Childs Way. Turn right signposted Willen Lake, under the H6, ahead at the next footpath junction, under the second bridge and immediately right, signposted Kingston. You are now skirting South Willen Lake. Continue with the lake on your left, ignoring the path going under the road bridge into the poplar plantation; the walk passes through there shortly. This lake is a busy one for activities and

Poplar plantation and river Ouzel

you are likely to see craft on the water and walkers and joggers on the lakeside paths. In a short distance, the path forks, the right hand fork climbing to the road. Take the left fork here and then right at a signpost to go under the H6 along the banks of the River Ouzel.

You will pass a sign indicating that you are now in the Ouzel Valley Park and the path goes along by the river with the poplar plantation on your right, a very attractive spot. Cross the bridge over the Ouzel and turn right, so that the river is now on your right and go under V10 Brickhill Street. It may be a bit muddy here after rain. The path goes slightly away from the water here through meadowland. There is a path to the left rising to a viewpoint with benches, which is worth the short detour for the attractive view.

Return to the path and go left to continue to a footpath crossroads. Go right here to cross the bridge over the river and turn left on to the path near the water. There are allotments on your right. Go through a double gate to follow the river, now on your left. Cross a bridge over a ditch and continue alongside the water. Soon you will come to the site of a medieval manor and fishponds dating from the fourteenth century, with an information board explaining what the bumps in the ground signify.

After going through another gate, the path follows the meandering of the river, with meadowland on the right. Go through another double gate to go under H7 Chaffron Way, ahead through yet another gate, ignoring the path to the right, and follow the path as it curves left. There is a wooden bridge on your left. Do not cross this but go through another gate and ahead. The path loops away from the river, then rejoins it and meanders alongside it. There are more gates on this section and there may be sheep grazing in the meadows.

After a while the path curves away from the river and you reach a junction of footpaths. Go ahead here, signposted Woughton. The path you are on is soon joined by another path coming from the bridge on your left. The path then curves right and you can see Woughton church tower in the distance and the dome of Xscape way over to the right. Go over a boarded section. There are playing fields now ahead to your left. A path joins from the right, go through a gate, over a footbridge and turn right, signposted The Green. Continue on this path until you see a gate on the right.

Take the path that goes off to the left here and runs alongside the playing field and out on to the road. This path too may be muddy after rain and its surface is not as good as the rest of the walk. If you prefer, you can continue to the end of the path you are on instead of taking the path to the left round the playing field, in which case you will emerge in Lucas Place and proceed left along it to its junction with the road, where you will see the Olde Swan pub. Turn left at the road and take the next path on the right.

If you have taken the path round the playing fields, when you come out on to the road, the Olde Swan pub is a little way along on your right. Go left and cross the road to take the path almost ahead.

You are now on the path taking you into the Community Orchard, where at the right time of year you might want to sample the free apples. Go through the orchard, ignoring the track to the left and a crossing track but going right where a path goes off to the right over a footbridge and brings you out on the Green. At the road, turn right, then left and pick up the first path that

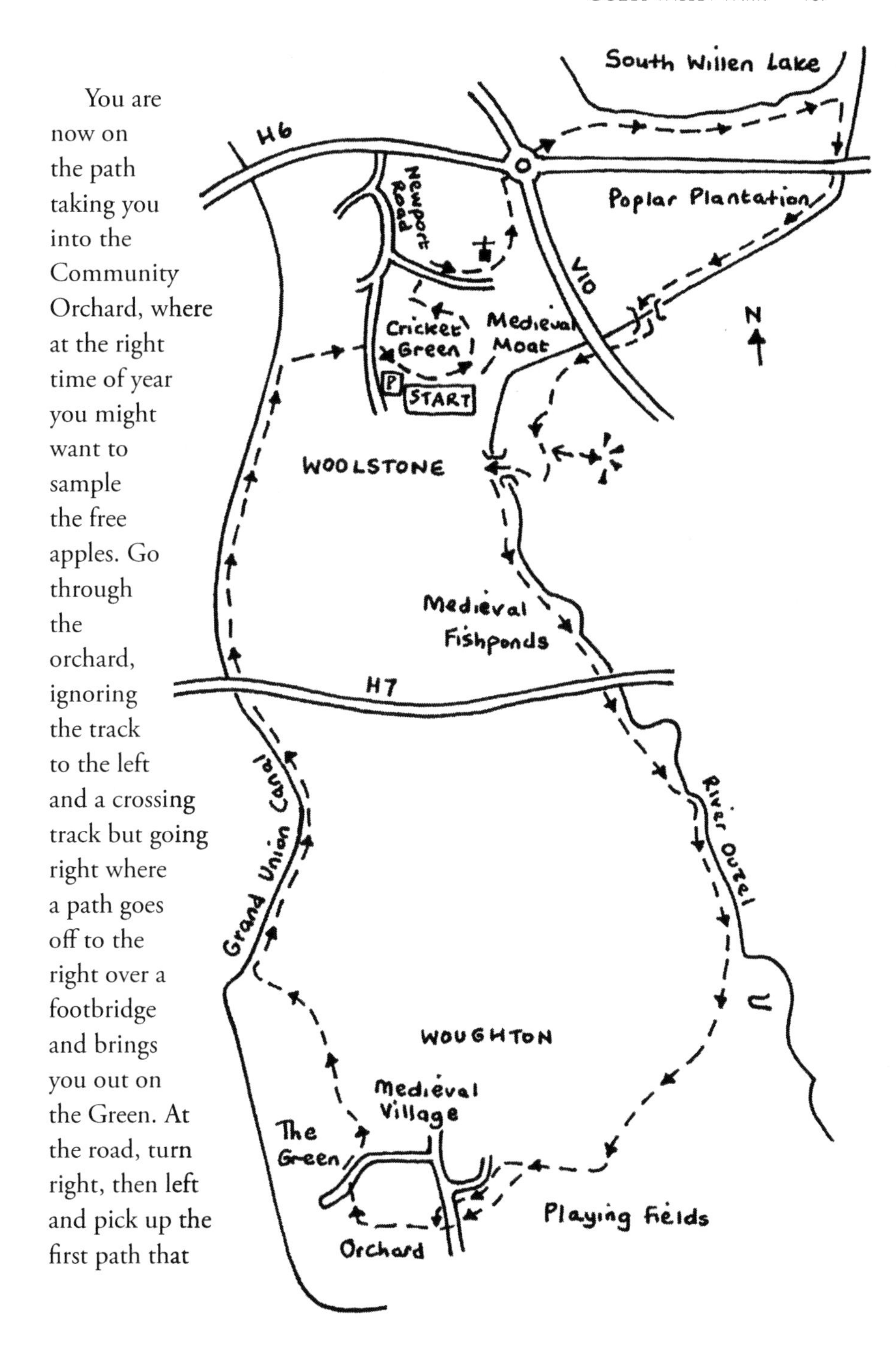

Idyllic scene in the Ouzel Valley Park

goes right off this road as it curves round the green. The junction of this footpath with the road is a good place to stop and look at the Green, an attractive spot. The area in front of the church is the site of a medieval village.

Continue ahead on the Millennium Cycle route. Cross a minor road and you will soon see a bridge over the Grand Union canal ahead of you. Ignoring the path to the right, go up to the bridge but turn right before it to pick up the canal broadwalk. This is a wide, often poplar-lined path that runs alongside the canal as it passes through the city. Continue on the broadwalk with paddocks on the right, ignoring crossing paths. Go under Chaffron Way H7 and, ignoring the footpath on the right at the far side of the bridge, take the third footpath on the right after this, which slopes down past some houses. Cross a minor road, go past a play area on the left, cross another road and curve right to get back to the car park.

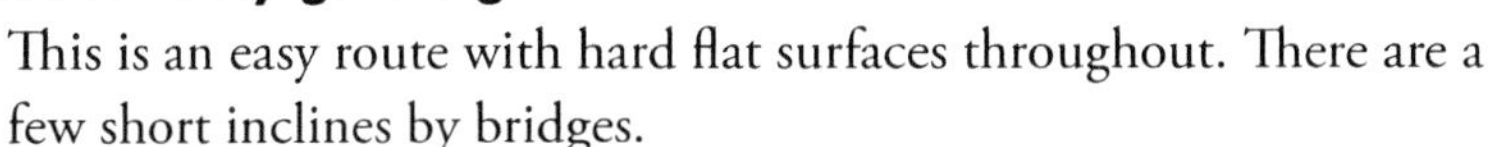

Canal Broadwalk

Accessibility grading

This is an easy route with hard flat surfaces throughout. There are a few short inclines by bridges.

Distance

A linear route of some three and a half miles. You can make it as short or as long as you like up to seven miles, by retracing your steps at any point.

Directions and Parking

The walk starts from the Ouzel Valley car park opposite the water garden at Woughton on the Green. It is off Newport road just south of Chaffron Way H7 between Marlborough Street V8 and Brickhill Street V10. Note that there is an entrance height barrier to the car park of 6'3" (1.90m).

Refreshments and Facilities

There is a pub restaurant on the route at Gifford Park, which has toilets with disabled access. There is also a café just off the route between H4 and H5 at Camphill, which is accessible to wheels but does not currently have toilets with wheelchair access.

Points of Interest

This walk explores the canal broadwalk starting from Woughton on the Green up to Great Linford Park. The Grand Union canal weaves through Milton Keynes in a broad arc from Old Wolverton in the Ouse Valley Park in the north of the city to Water Eaton in Bletchley in the south. As well as being a reminder of the area's industrial past, it is also a haven for wildlife and gives many opportunities for leisure activities. The canal broadwalk, a firm, wide path managed by the Parks Trust, runs from Linford Manor Park in the north of the city south to Woughton on the Green, a distance of some three and a half miles. It is suitable for wheelchairs and pushchairs and runs within sight of the canal all the way. There is a towpath nearer the water but this is quite narrow and not suitable for wheels. However, the water can always be seen from the broadwalk, often glimpsed through poplar trees lining the route, and there are some stretches without trees giving an uninterrupted view of the canal.

The walk includes colourful narrow boats moored or travelling at a sedate pace along the waterway, attractive old bridges and a wealth of wild life, especially waterfowl. An attractive feature of most of the walk is the poplars lining both sides of the route and there are often squirrels scampering around them and birds singing in the trees and bushes.

Along the route is the proposed start point for the link between the Grand Union Canal and the River Great Ouse, first suggested as long ago as 1811, and now with a target opening date of 2010. It will be the first new canal scheme in a hundred years. The new canal will be approximately 20 miles long and will bring many benefits to the local economy, improving the landscape, creating new wildlife habitats and providing local people and visitors with new sport and leisure activities.

THE WALK

Leave the car park through the double gate to the left of the cattle grid, turn left and cross the road to go ahead over a footbridge. There is a wider access path to the right but you will need to go left immediately to join the correct path. You are now on a path with the water garden on your right. You will pass paddocks on your left and later too on the right. Ignore any paths going to the left and continue ahead. After a while, the path curves right to go over a bridge over the canal. Turn right before the bridge and you are now on the canal broadwalk.

When you reach the canal, you will keep it on your left all the way out and on your right on the way back except for the last stretch

Peaceful canalside scene

through Great Linford Park where you will cross over to the other side of the water. Unless the directions state otherwise, you should always continue ahead at any crossroads of footpaths and at bridges.

You will see first a play area and later paddocks on your right, and will soon pass under Chaffron Way H7, where the route becomes more wooded.

After a while you pass under Childs Way H6 and on one of the two bridges there is an interesting sign stating that the Bedford and Milton Keynes Waterway will start on the right just north of here. Just after you pass under the bridge there is a wooden sign by the canal bank, saying simply 'To Bedford', referring to this proposed link between the Grand Union Canal and the River Great Ouse. For more details see the Points of Interest section. Soon you will see Campbell Park on the other side of the canal, recognisable by its

Waterbirds on Grand Union Canal

huge statue of a head. When you come to the next bridge over the canal, do not cross the bridge but take either of the two routes to continue ahead, the lower one being flatter but with a slope at the end. This is a popular mooring spot for narrowboats.

Pass under Portway H5, into a more open section, which soon becomes tree-lined again. You will pass a large running track and a path going to the right, which you should ignore. At the next old bridge, there is a play area on the other side of the canal. The road to the right here leads in a very short distance to Camphill Café (see Refreshments section).

Soon after this, there is a play area on the right, then the path goes left, then zigzags over a boarded section. At the end of the boarded section turn left to come back alongside the canal, still with the canal on your left. Continue and pass under Dansteed Way H4.

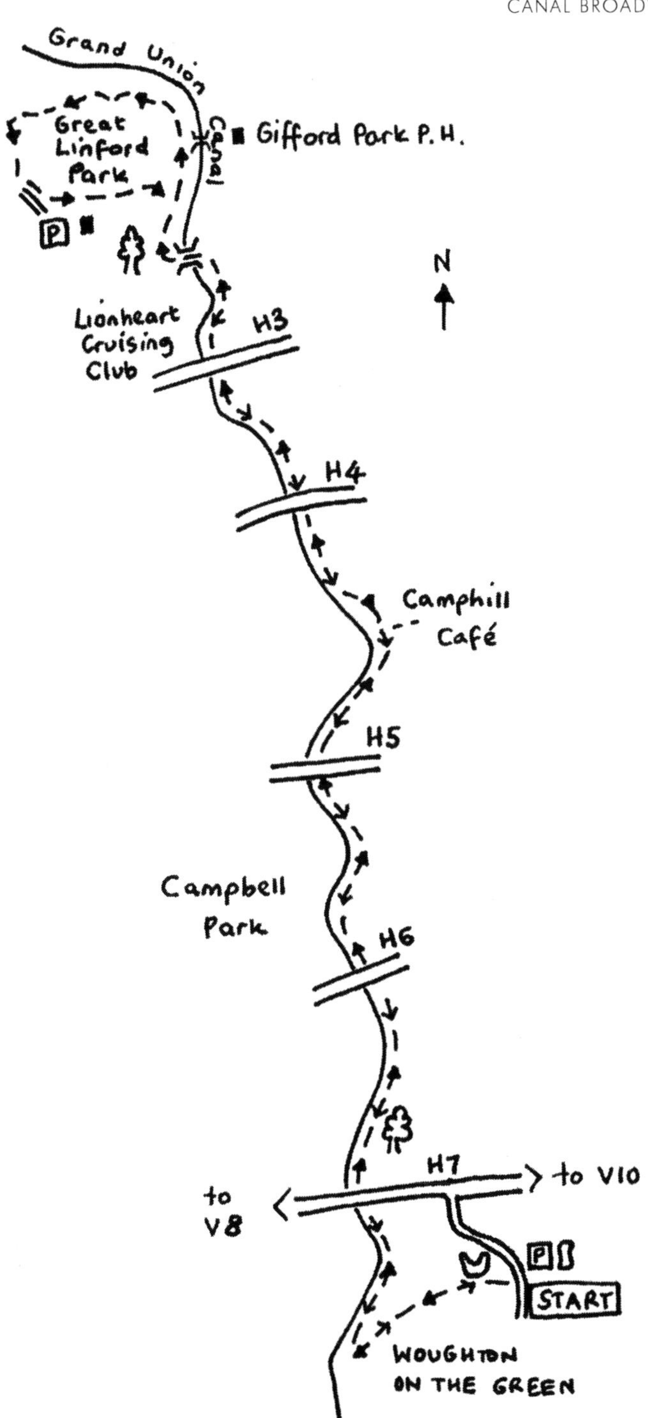
Grand Union Canal
Gifford Park P.H.
Great Linford Park
P
N
Lionheart Cruising Club
H3
H4
Camphill Café
H5
Campbell Park
H6
H7
to V10
to V8
P
START
WOUGHTON ON THE GREEN

Notice the wooden bridge on the other side of the canal, leading to a private section of water.

After you go under Monks Way H3, you will go past the Lionheart Cruising Club, where more boats are moored. At the second bridge the broadwalk no longer continues on the right hand side of the canal. Instead the path goes under the bridge, then curves right to go up and over it to continue on the left side of the canal. Cross the bridge and turn right to have the water on your right for the last stretch.

The paddocks on your left soon give way to Great Linford Park. Continue along the edge of the park towards the bridge. There is a pub restaurant, Gifford Park, on the other side of the bridge, so if you want to go there, cross the bridge and follow the ramp round to the front of the building. Otherwise bear left before the bridge to continue alongside the water. The path curves gently away from the canal between fences; this is a quiet and peaceful stretch. When you come to a road, turn left for a short distance on a path running alongside the road, then left down a minor road towards a car park. Take the first path to the left before the car park to go back through the middle of Great Linford Park, past the sports fields. When you see the bridge ahead of you, take the right fork to pick up the canal side again and begin your return journey.

When retracing your steps, remember that the canal is on your left to start, then remains on your right after crossing the first bridge until the end of the walk. Take care too to turn right over the boarded section between H4 and H5.

Furzton and Teardrop Lakes

Accessibility grading 

The route is on hard tracks all the way, with two fairly steep slopes, which can be avoided if necessary.

Distance

A circular walk of about 3½ miles, with two options for a shorter distance.

Option 1. Starting from the lakeside car park that is just off Watling Street V4 between the Elfield Park and the Bowl roundabouts gives a distance of about 3 miles and is a good alternative, if you need to avoid the steep hill near the beginning of the walk. Note that this car park has an entrance height barrier of 6'3" (1.90m).

Option 2. A walk around Furzton Lake itself is about 1½ miles.

Directions and Parking

The walk starts from Furzton Lake, which lies to the southwest of Watling Street V4 between Chaffron Way H7 and Standing Way H8. There are two parking areas round the lake, either of which could be used as a starting point. However, the walk is described from the car park reached by taking the H7 south from the Bowl roundabout on the V4, and following the car park signs.

Refreshments and Facilities

The Travel Inn to the north of the lake is a good place to stop for refreshments. To reach it with wheels, go past the narrow boat moored on the water to the right and in front of the pub. There are ramps on this side, whereas there are steps if you approach on the left. The pub is accessible for wheelchairs and has a toilet suitable for disabled users.

Points of Interest

This walk is very varied and includes Furzton Lake, the Milton Keynes Bowl, and Teardrop Lakes.

Furzton Lake is one of Milton Keynes' balancing lakes, which were created in the 1980s to retain water during periods of heavy rain to prevent flooding. It has a striking sculpture, the Triple Star Head, shaped like a comet, and wooden sculptures on the islands.

The Bowl is a major entertainment venue famous for its open-air concerts. It is a massive venue, which can hold 65,000 people. In 1992 a huge sound stage was added, which has since enabled it to attract some major stars, such as David Bowie, Michael Jackson, Bon Jovi and Robbie Williams.

Teardrop Lakes are an attractive string of four connecting teardrop-shaped lakes. They are a haven for wildlife as they provide an ideal habitat for waterfowl.

THE WALK

Leaving the car park, go down to the lake, turn left with the water on your right and follow the curve of the lake round past the Travel Inn. Lots of geese and mallard congregate here as people tend to feed them, but the lake is a haven for all sorts of waterfowl. Follow the path as it curves to the right and ignore paths to the left. Then there is a steep slope down and up again (avoidable by doing Option 1 – see Distance section), followed by a gentle climb to a higher spot near the Triple Star Head sculpture overlooking the lake, from where you have a lovely view over the water.

Turn left just before the sculpture to go towards the road bridge, passing the Watling Street car park. If you are doing Option 1 above, turn right on leaving the car park and start following the directions from here.

Cross the bridge to go over Watling Street V4. Go left down the minor road and briefly ahead on to the Redway alongside Watling Street V4, before following Route 51 as it branches right. This path takes you round the Milton Keynes Bowl. Go left over a bridge and immediately right to go alongside a stream on your right. The path follows the stream as it goes round the Bowl and the coach park and crosses a couple of minor roads before reaching Chaffron Way H7.

Go under H7 and ahead, ignoring the path to the left. Here the stream soon becomes the first of the Teardrop Lakes and you enter a different world, away from the hustle and bustle of the city. You may see a solitary heron standing guard over the water as well as swans, mallard, great crested grebe, moorhen and coot.

Continue ahead, keeping to the left of all lakes. However, it is worth going on to the bridges that cross the streams separating the four lakes to enjoy or capture the views. Some of these bridges are also very attractive structures. Each little lake seems to have its own character; one is heavily fringed with rushes, another may have a few fishermen enjoying the peaceful setting, on another you may watch

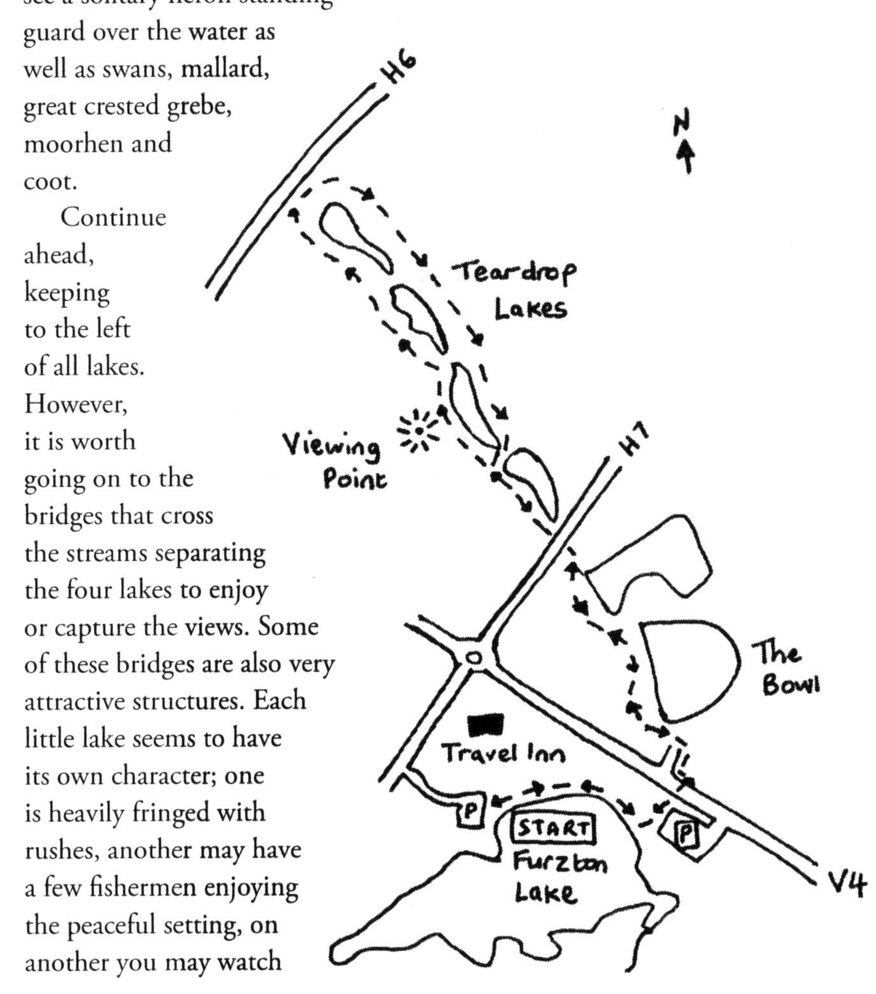

A heron stands guard over one of the Teardrop lakes

grebes diving under water in front of you or a moorhen scuttling away at your approach.

When you come to the end of the lakes you will see Childs Way H6 ahead of you. Turn right before the steps to go round the head of the lakes. Go ahead across the straight side of the large semicircular structure jutting out towards the lake. There is a short ramp to get on and off this structure. Do not go round the semicircular path, as there is a large raised metal cover half way round. Descend the slope and on your left you will see a tunnel under the road bridge but do not go under it: instead, ascend the opposite slope and curve round the top of the lake. If you find this structure too difficult to negotiate, retrace your route back down the same side of the lakes, instead of crossing over to the other side, and follow the instructions in the final paragraph.

You will now return down the other side of the first three lakes,

A peaceful scene on one of the Teardrop lakes

keeping to the main path, Route 51, rather than the bridleway that runs nearer the water. Notice how some of the lakes look different from the other side. For example, the top lake has lots of rushes on this side, which obscure the view of the water. Alongside the third lake you pass, the path curves right and crosses the bridleway, which veers away from the lakes at this point. Here you should cross the bridge to the other side of the lakes, staying on Route 51 to go down the final lake with the water on your left.

From this point, retrace your outward route, going past the first lake, under the road bridge, past the Bowl, following the Route 51 signs all the way, but making sure you go right towards Furzton Lake not left where Route 51 goes in both directions. If you are parked in the alternative car park, you will pass this first, otherwise continue going right when you get to the lake and follow the path round to the car park.

Furzton Lake and Emerson Valley

Accessibility grading ⊛⊛

Easy terrain throughout, with hard, mainly flat surfaces all the way. The route is graded two wheels because there are some inclines.

Distance

A circular walk of about 5½ miles, or 4½ using the alternative car park.

Another option from this starting point is a walk around Furzton Lake itself, which is about one and a half miles.

Directions and Parking

Furzton Lake lies to the southwest of Watling Street V4 between Chaffron Way H7 and Standing Way H8. There are two parking areas round the lake, either of which can be used as a starting point for this walk. The route is described from the car park reached by taking the H7 south from the Bowl roundabout on the V4, and following the car park signs.

The other car park is just off V4 Watling Street between the Elfield Park and the Bowl roundabouts. Note that this car park has a height barrier of 6'3" (1.90m). The route description shows where you can join and leave the walk using this car park. This makes the walk about a mile shorter and avoids the steep slope near the beginning of the walk.

Refreshments and Facilities

The Travel Inn to the north of the lake is a good place to stop for refreshments. To reach it with wheels, go past the narrow boat moored on the water to the right of the pub. There are ramps on this side, whereas there are steps if you approach on the left. The pub is accessible for wheelchairs and has a toilet suitable for disabled users.

Points of Interest

This walk goes round Furzton Lake and through Emerson Valley Park. It also takes in Howe Park Wood, a Site of Special Scientific Interest (SSSI).

Furzton Lake is one of Milton Keynes' balancing lakes, which were created in the 1980s to retain water during periods of heavy rain to prevent flooding. It has a striking sculpture, the Triple Star Head, shaped like a comet, and wooden sculptures on the islands.

Emerson Valley is a residential area, which takes its name from two nearby farms, Emerson Farm and Valley Farm. The route follows the brook that runs through parkland in the middle of Emerson Valley and is very attractive, especially in spring.

Howe Park Wood is an ancient woodland, probably mentioned in the Doomsday Book, and designated an SSSI because of its nationally important species of plants and animals. It was bought by Milton Keynes Development Corporation in 1968, opened up to provide a variety of habitats for wildlife and is now managed using traditional methods such as coppicing. The wood is an especially lovely place to visit in spring for its birdsong and carpets of wild flowers and in summer for the many different butterflies in the glades and open paths, including unusual ones such as the White Admiral, the Wood White and the Purple Hairstreak. There are more than 200 plant species in the wood, including rare ones, and some fine old trees. Many birds breed here, such as Green and Greater-spotted Woodpecker, Tree Creeper, Willow Warbler, Sparrowhawk and Tawny Owl.

THE WALK

Leaving the car park, go down to the lake, turn left with the water on your right and follow the curve of the lake round past the Travel Inn. Lots of geese and mallard congregate here as people tend to feed them, but the lake is a haven for all sorts of waterfowl. Follow the path as it curves right and ignore paths to the left. Then there is a steep slope down and up again (avoidable by using the alternative car park – see the Directions and Parking section), followed by a gentle climb to a higher spot at the Triple Star Head sculpture overlooking the lake, from where you have a lovely view over the water.

If you have started from the alternative car park, go towards the Triple Star Head sculpture until you can see the lake and turn left with the water on your right, then start following the instructions from here.

Continue with the lake on your right and a wooden bridge ahead. Turn left before the bridge, ignoring the path going immediately left from this one going back towards the sculpture, and follow the path past a smaller lake on your right. Turn right across a wooden bridge then ahead to go alongside a hedge, ignoring

Swans in Emerson Valley

Triple Star Head sculpture

the path to your right as you leave the bridge. There are allotments on the far side of this hedge.

Follow the path as it bears right through a local park. When the path forks, take the right hand route. When you pass a signpost near a children's playground, follow the direction Emerson Valley Park. Ignore any crossing paths until you come to a fork, where you should take the right path over the bridge into a local park to join Route 51.

Go left, keeping the stream on your right. Cross a road and follow the path as it bears first left and then right, ignoring the path to the left going towards the houses. This is a pretty section of the stream, often alive with birdsong. Follow Route 51 as it goes right again over a bridge and you will still have a stream on your right. Cross a minor road and a footbridge under Fulmer Street V3.

The path curves right to follow the stream along another pretty stretch of the route. There are bulrushes along the water's edge, little waterfalls and bridges and lots of coot and moorhen. Cross a road and go past a little lake and follow the meandering stream with more waterfalls and water birds.

Go under Tattenhoe Street V2 and continue past yet more waterfalls, ignoring the bridges crossing the stream and any crossing paths. Look out for a pagoda on the far side of the stream.

Shortly after passing the pagoda, you will come to a Redway that crosses the route at a sign indicating Loughton Valley Park and Tattenhoe Valley. You will be able to see a large industrial-looking building ahead and to your left at this point. Go right on this Redway and cross the bridge. Continue to the roundabout, where you should bear right into Hartland Avenue. When you reach St Ives Crescent, turn left on to the Redway that runs through the middle, a long steady climb. The path goes past the houses, through a district park and curves right to meet a road. Turn left along the road – this is a quiet road but take care – for a short distance, taking the first right fork into Hengistbury Lane.

On the right you will see a bridleway marker by a gravel circle with trees in the middle and a gate at the back. Go through this gate into parkland and bear left to follow the path going through Howe Park Wood. Follow the main track through the wood, enjoying the change in scenery from streamside to woodland. Go through the gate to leave the wood, leading to a bridge over Tattenhoe Street V2, which has a fairly steep slope up to it.

You will see a 'roundabout' where several paths meet. Go right and take the second exit to follow the left hand edge of a district park. Cross another path at a staggered junction and keep going ahead, ignoring paths to left and right. You will see a grassy mound on your left. Go under a wooden archway and turn left at the roadside approaching this mound. Turn right at the mound and take the second exit, a right turn towards Furzton, through a local park with a playground on your right.

You will then come to Rusland Circus, another grassy mound with a path running round the base. Turn right to go round it and take the path to the right between Hodder Lane and Hawkshead Drive. This path goes over a bridge, which climbs to

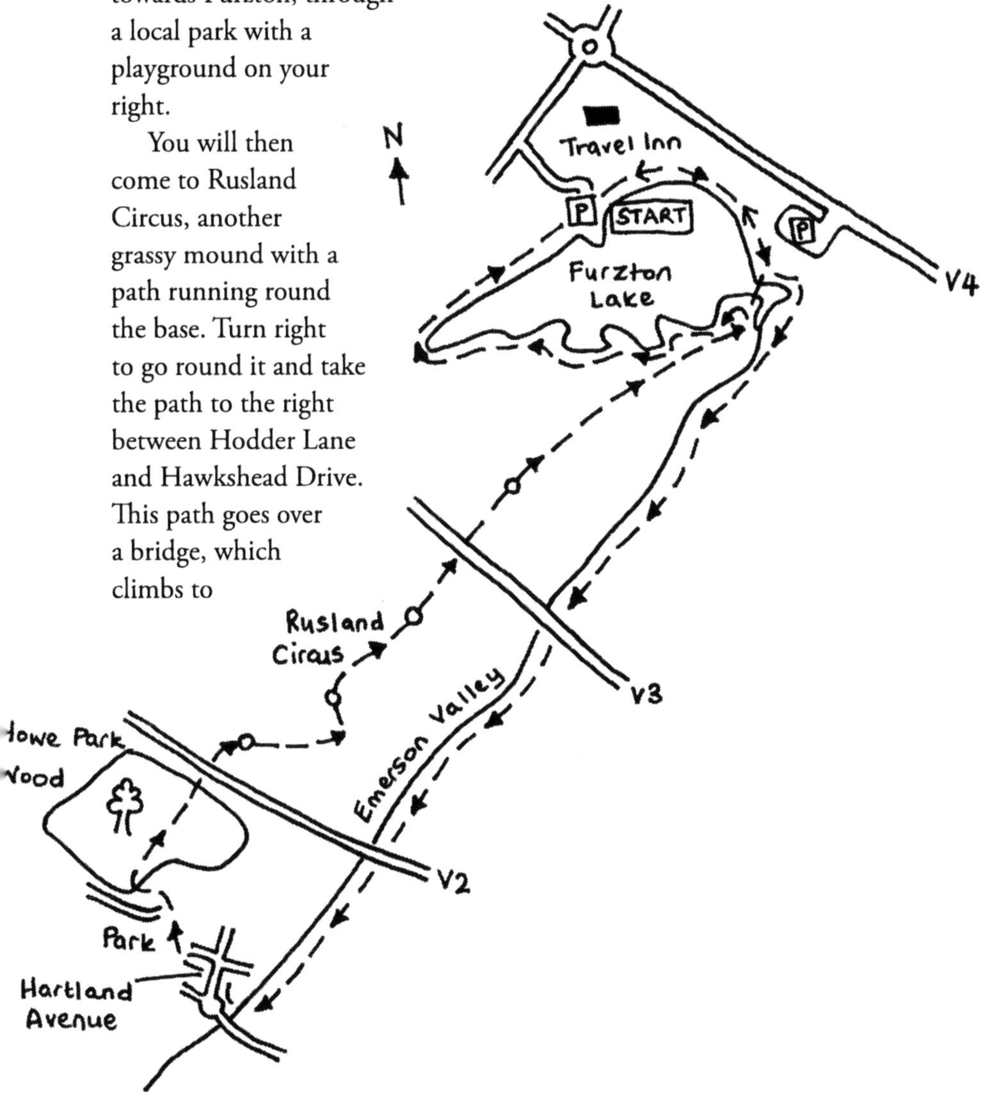

Howe Park Wood

go over Fulmer Street V3. The route is signposted Elfield Park and the Bowl. You pass another grassy mound on your left as you go through a local park. Continue on this strip of parkland between houses until you pass a sports centre and come to Furzton Lake.

If you have used the alternative car park, you are nearly back. Go over the bridge and bear right after the sculpture, until you reach the car park.

If you want to get back quickly at this point, cross the bridge and go left round the northern shore, retracing the route you took at the start of the walk. Otherwise, turn left before the bridge and follow the lakeside path as it zigzags round the southern shore of the lake. This is a very attractive part of the walk, quieter than the northern shore and it is possible to get closer to the water birds here, perhaps watching a heron catch a fish or a grebe diving. After about a mile, look out for the car park on the left.

Caldecotte Lake

Accessibility grading

This is an easy route with hard flat surfaces throughout, using mainly Leisure routes with a short section of Redway.

Distance

A circular walk of about 4 miles.

Directions and Parking

Caldecotte Lake lies north and south of Bletcham Way H10 between Brickhill Street V10 and the A5. There are several parking areas round the lake, but this walk starts from the car park on the south lake, off Monellan Grove, just south of the H10 between the Walton Park and Caldecotte roundabouts. The car park is on the right just after Caldecotte Lane on the left.

Refreshments and Facilities

The Caldecotte Arms on the north lake is about halfway round the route. It is accessible for wheelchairs and has toilets suitable for disabled users. It also has parking bays specially designated for disabled people and you could start and end the walk there if you wished, adjusting the directions accordingly.

Points of Interest

The walk is very varied and includes the north and south lakes, and the sites of a medieval moat and fishponds and of a sixteenth century manor. It is divided between lakeside and meadowland.

Caldecotte Lake was named after the medieval settlement on this site. It was excavated between 1981 and 1983 from farmland on either side of the river Ouzel, in order to store excess rainwater and prevent flooding. It comprises two lakes and is popular for all types of sports and leisure activities. Because of its size, however, it is possible to get away to more peaceful spots. The lakes are home to a rich variety of wildfowl, because much of the land used to be wetland and marsh before it was drained for agriculture. Some are permanent inhabitants, some are temporary visitors and some are introduced species that have settled here. You can expect to see lots of waterfowl and other birds, as well as sheep on the medieval sites.

The Caldecotte Arms pub was purpose-built as a windmill and is an attractive feature visible from several points on the walk.

This is an area rich in **medieval remains** and on this walk you will pass the site of a moat and fishponds. You will also pass the site of a sixteenth century manor.

THE WALK

From the car park, go down to the lake and turn left. You will keep the lake on your right all the time you are alongside it. Although the path is always wide, it sometimes runs quite close to the edge, so take care. It also moves away from the lake at times, which adds variety to the views. In a short while turn left away from the lake where the path curves round in front of an attractive crescent of buildings, following the water's edge. As you approach the water sports club on the other side of the crescent, take the Redway to the left just before the end of the crescent, go past the club buildings and turn right afterwards to bring you back to the water's edge again.

You now pass over a boarded bridge. Continue to follow the path past some buildings and if you like, take the path which loops right towards the lake- there is a bird hide down here and seats by the water - then left and left again before turning right to rejoin the main path. If you decide not to take the loop, simply continue on the main path, as it goes round the southern edge of the lake. Here it veers away from the water a little way and you find yourself among trees and grassy areas with only glimpses of water. The railway line passes by overhead to your left.

Here there is another loop from the main trail, which is worth

Reflections on Caldecotte Lake

taking. It turns right towards the water and passes another bird hide, where there is a poster showing wildfowl you might see here, such as coot, moorhen, goldeneye, pochard, little and great crested grebe, tufted duck and mallard. You might like to stop for a while to see how many different species you can spot. Follow the path round and turn right to regain the main route round the bottom of the lake.

As you turn to come up the side of the water, you will notice a bridge on the left over the river Ouzel. Do not take this, but continue ahead alongside and now slightly above the water. There are good views in all directions on this stretch, with the windmill of the Caldecotte Arms ahead of you and the landmarks you passed on the other side of the lake visible across the water. Ignore the signpost marked 'North Lake' to the left, as we are taking a different route to the other part of the lake. Continue ahead, following the path along the lake and under Bletcham Way H10 to come out in front of the Caldecotte Arms. This would be a good chance to have a break and refreshments if you wished. If you decided to start and end your

Rural scene near medieval sites

walk at the pub, then follow the directions from this point, with the lake on your right.

Follow the path close to the water's edge, keeping to the inside of the posts for safety reasons. Here there is a spit of land going out into the lake and the path goes around it. At its point, the area has a more remote feel, with lots of wildfowl. As you round the point back towards the pub, you will see a weir on your right and soon after a path leading to a bridge on your left. Take this path and cross the bridge over the river Ouzel, then turn right and go to the T-junction, with the weir on your right.

The path to the left takes you to the sites of a medieval moat and fishponds and of a sixteenth century manor. Turn left, then shortly right through two gates on to a surfaced path over fields. This is a very attractive rural scene, with a church in the distance and often with sheep in the fields, very different from a few minutes earlier. However, sheep in the fields means the paths may not be as clean

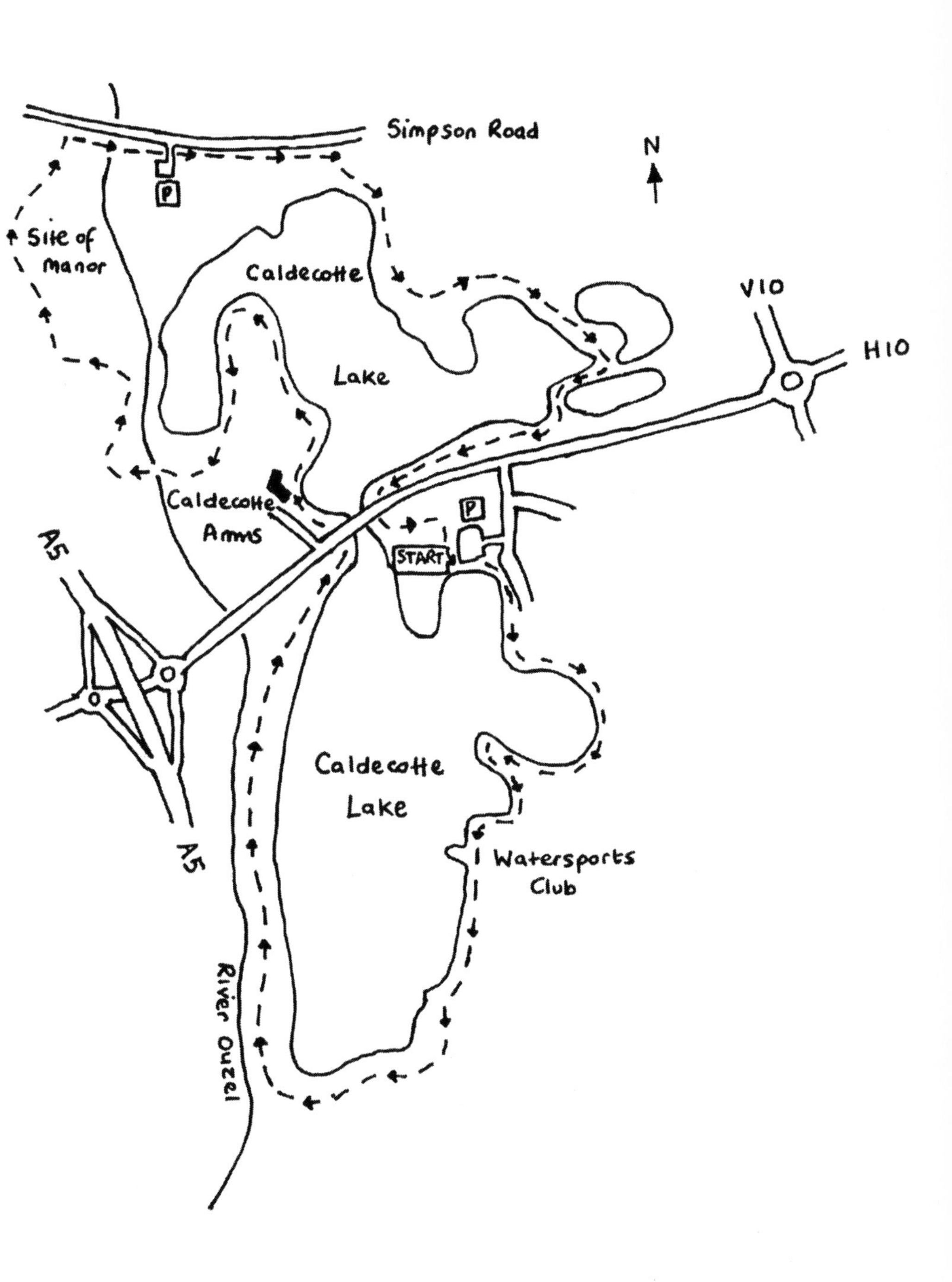
Simpson Road
N
P
Site of
Manor
Caldecotte
Lake
V10
H10
Caldecotte
Arms
P
START
A5
A5
Caldecotte
Lake
Watersports
Club
River Ouzel

as on the rest of the walk! You can see the hollows where the moat and fishponds were and there is a good view of the windmill of the Caldecotte Arms in the distance across the fields. The path curves to the right past the site of the sixteenth century manor, which is marked out in stones, showing quite clearly the position of the rooms. There are benches here and a picnic table, a very attractive spot to spend some time. Go through the gate and over the bridge across a stream and go right along the Redway.

You are now going level with the road and a bridge takes you over the river Ouzel once more. A bridleway runs close to the path you are on for some distance now, but the main path has a better surface. Continue, enjoying the views over the lake beyond the grassy area on your right. As this grassy area ends, take the path to your right. The path climbs to the left, then turns to run alongside the lake. Keep to the path near the lake rather than the bridleway that runs alongside. Soon you will see a short spur off to a sitting area overlooking the lake, which you might wish to take to enjoy the views and the waterfowl. The path shortly curves left away from the water, but almost immediately meets the lake again at a very pretty spot, where you can follow the water's edge along a boardwalk. You may be rewarded by the sight of a heron here, perhaps feeding on fish or flapping away majestically at your approach. Follow the path round in front of some houses and go down to a further boardwalk by another tranquil stretch of water, surrounded by rushes. This is a lovely area with water all around where you might see a great-crested grebe diving and resurfacing. Retrace your steps to the main path and continue past a pagoda and over a bridge.

Turn right to follow the path round the lake and for a short distance you have water on both sides of you. Go over another bridge and the path curves right, following the road. On this stretch, you can glimpse through the trees a floating pontoon, often covered in cormorants. Soon you will see the pub opposite, and the path goes under the road and curves round, going over a bridge to reach the car park.

CIRCULAR WALKS ALONG THE CHILTERN WAY
Volume One Buckinghamshire & Oxfordshire
Volume Two Hertfordshire & Bedfordshire

Nick Moon

A two-volume series with special maps provided for each walk.

The walks range from 4.3 to 8.8 miles which makes for a comfortable half day or a leisurely full day walk. In addition, details of several possible combinations of walks of up to 22 miles are provided for those who would like a longer, more challenging walk.

Each walk gives details of nearby places of interest and is accompanied by a specially drawn map of the route which also indicates local pubs and a skeleton road network.

CHILTERN WALKS
Hertfordshire, Bedfordshire and North Buckinghamshire

CHILTERN WALKS
Buckinghamshire

CHILTERN WALKS
Oxfordshire and West Buckinghamshire

Nick Moon

A series of three books to providing a comprehensive coverage of walks throughout the whole of the Chiltern area (as defined by the Chiltern Society). The walks included vary in length from 3.0 to 10.9 miles, but are mainly in the 5–7 mile range popular for half-day walks, although suggestions of possible combinations of walks are given for those preferring a full day's walk.

Each walk gives details of nearby places of interest and is accompanied by a specially drawn map of the route which also indicates local pubs and a skeleton road network.

FAMILY WALKS
Chilterns – South

FAMILY WALKS
Chilterns – North

Nick Moon

A series of two books, providing a comprehensive coverage of walks throughout the whole of the Chiltern area. The walks included vary in length from 1.7 to 5.5 miles, but are mainly in the 3 to 5 mile range, which is ideal for families with children, less experienced walkers or short winter afternoons.

Each walk text gives details of nearby places of interest and is accompanied by a specially drawn map of the route, which also indicates local pubs and a skeleton road network.

The author, Nick Moon, has lived in or regularly visited the Chilterns all his life and has for 25 years, been an active member of the Chiltern Society's Rights of Way Group, which seeks to protect and improve the area's footpath and bridleway network.

THE CHILTERN AREA'S LEADING SERIES OF MAPS FOR WALKERS
by Nick Moon

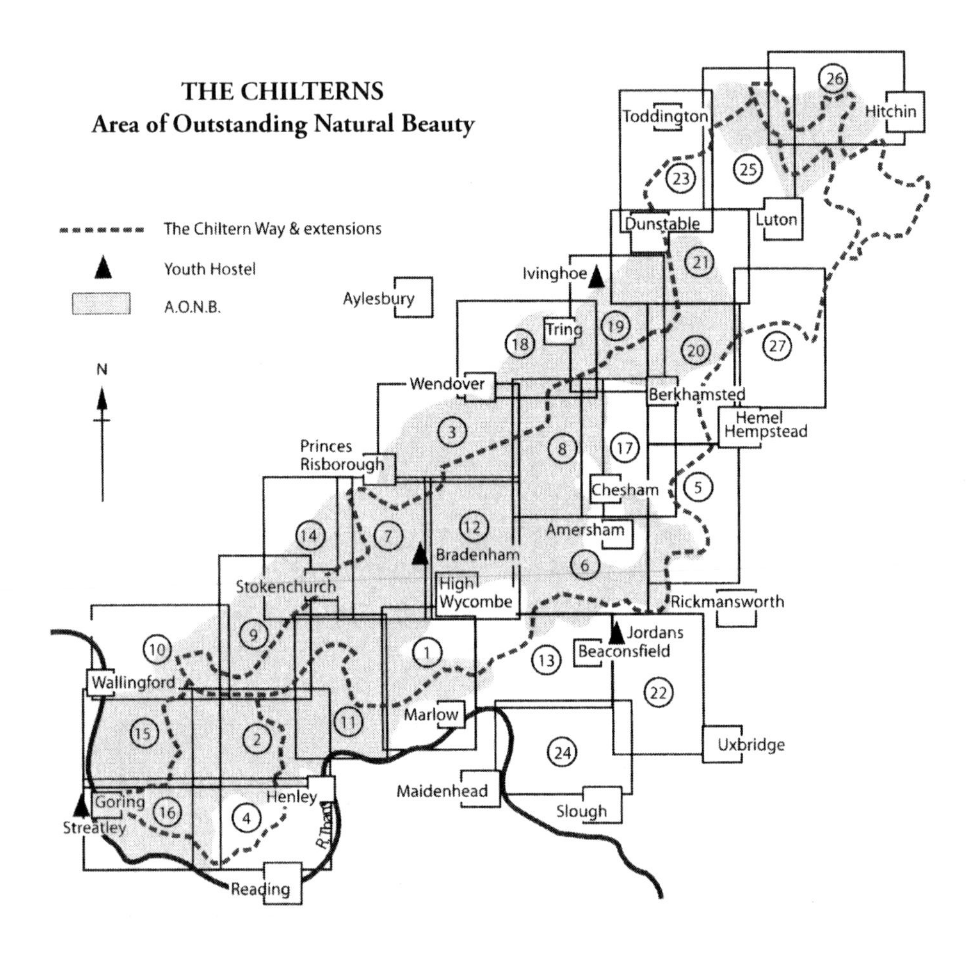

This expanding series of currently 27 maps at a scale of 2½ inches to the mile depicts footpaths, bridleways and other routes available to walkers, riders and cyclists across the Chilterns, as well as pubs, railway stations, car parking facilities and other features of interest. Several suggested walks also appear on the back of each map. New titles appear regularly and will soon extend coverage from the Thames in the south to Hitchin in the north.

COMPLETE LIST OF CHILTERN SOCIETY FOOTPATH MAPS

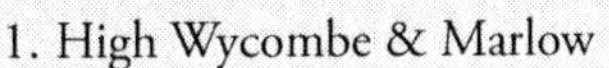

1. High Wycombe & Marlow
2. Henley & Nettlebed
3. Wendover & Princes Risborough
4. Henley & Caversham
5. Sarratt & Chipperfield
6. Amersham & Penn Country
7. West Wycombe & Princes Risborough
8. Chartridge & Cholesbury
9. The Oxfordshire Escarpment
10. Wallingford & Watlington
11. The Hambleden Valley
12. Hughenden Valley & Gt.Missenden
13. Beaconsfield & District
14. Stokenchurch & Chinnor
15. Crowmarsh & Nuffield
16. Goring & Mapledurham
17. Chesham & Berkhamsted
18. Tring & Wendover
19. Ivinghoe & Ashridge
20. Hemel Hempstead & the Gade Valley
21. Dunstable Downs & Caddington
22. Gerrards Cross & Chalfont St.Peter
23. Toddington & Houghton Regis
24. Burnham Beeches and Stoke Poges
25. Sundon and the Barton Hills
26. Hitchin and Hexton
27. Flamstead and Redbourn

Others in preparation

EXPLORING HISTORY ALL AROUND

Vivienne Evans

A handbook of local history, arranged as a series of routes to cover Bedfordshire and adjoining parts of Hertfordshire and Buckinghamshire. It is organised as two books in one. There are seven thematic sections full of fascinating historical detail and anecdotes for armchair reading. Also it is a perfect source of family days out as the book is organised as circular motoring/cycling explorations, highlighting attractions and landmarks. Also included is a background history to all the major towns in the area, plus dozens of villages, which will enhance your appreciation and understanding of the history that is all around you!